Jane Austen and the Irish Connection

By

Julia Forsythe

ACKNOWLEDGMENTS

My thanks to the following for their help.

The British Library, Camden Libraries, The Admiralty Library, Portsmouth, Hants. The National Archives, Kew, Richmond. Chawton House, Hampshire.

The Cork Library, Cork City and Harbour Archives. Christchurch Archives, Cork City. The Archives of 18th Century Maritime History, Cobh, Co. Cork.

To my friends, Ursula Morrissey who corrected the first draft of 'Sheridan' and to Domini Cline-Wilson for her invaluable help throughout the years. To Margaret O Neill for bringing me that particular Cork Examiner. To Darren Glynn, Maria Garcia and Josephine Siedleika for looking at various chapters for me. To my friends, Kathy Sheehy and Noreen Norman for coming with me to see places associated with Jane Austen. To Adrian for his help. To Mena who brought me to see Ballinamuck, in Co. Longford. To all my friends from Our Lady Help of Christians Church Kentish Town, and North London who listened to me over the years.

Finally, to my nieces and nephews, Jacinta who provided information on 'Fitzwilliam' Angela, Siobhan, Marian and Ted and all my relations who showed an interest. And to my Brother-in-Law Ted who came with me to Kinsale where we visited the "Stuart Forts". To my cousin, James Bacon, for his ideas.

Over time my son John helped and my son Paul checked over each chapter and finalised the book for publication. Lastly, I want to thank my brother John whose encouragement, patience and persistence kept me writing.

CHAPTER 1

ON THE ROAD TO WRITING THE BOOK

A journey of love began for me in 1995 as I watched the new BBC TV adaptation of Jane Austen's *Pride and Prejudice*. The handsome Colin Firth and beautiful Jennifer Ehle convincingly brought the characters of Fitzwilliam Darcy and Elizabeth Bennet to life and I quickly became enraptured in the romance, charm and eloquence of the series. Every Sunday night, on the phone between London and Cork, my sister Bernadette and I would enthusiastically dissect that evening's episode. Bernadette was undergoing chemotherapy at the time, and the romance of Darcy and Elizabeth was a distraction from its harsh side-effects. One evening she even took in a stray Golden Retriever and named him Darcy due to his gentle eyes. *Pride and Prejudice* soon became part of our dreams.

I became immersed in the world of Jane Austen and had soon read all but one of her novels. The final one I was reading was *Persuasion*, and even before finishing the first chapter I realised that I had read it before. I had since forgotten its title but had not forgotten the haunting quality of its writing, nor the details of how I happened upon it almost a lifetime ago...

...I was a young girl in Cork at the time. It was raining as I walked along Patrick Street and tripped over a brown paper bag with something inside it. I picked it up and tore open the soaking wet paper to find a book. A 'romance' I mused seeing the front cover then quickly put it under my plastic coat to keep it dry on the way home. It was to be the first "romance" that I had ever read...

This co-incidence of twice coming across the same book occupied my thoughts for many days after, and led to a growing passion for a better understanding of Jane's life and work. I had no knowledge of the internet at the time, so I began my quest the old-fashioned way, visiting bookshops and libraries across London to find anything written about Jane Austen.

Soon two more of Jane's novels, *Emma* and *Persuasion*, had been given new TV adaptations and were currently airing. The lines between London and Cork buzzed once again with excited discussion. Bernadette, who was an Irish dance teacher, could name some of the tunes featured in the dances. My son Paul also recognised the Irish traditional air, *The Dawning of the Day,* played on the piano by Jane Fairfax in *Emma*. I was surprised to hear of Irish music in such an English production. This surprise was compounded when, sometime later, browsing in a shop called Pastimes in Regent Street, I found a recently compiled book titled *Jane Austen's Music*. The book revealed that there were many Irish tunes and songs among Jane's manuscripts. The fact that Jane had played and sang music and songs that I had grown up with struck a chord with me and over time her music became one of my favourite subjects.

My sisters caught my passion for all things Jane Austen. Margaret and Bernadette regularly came to stay with me in Kentish Town and we had great fun touring the London of Jane's novels. I fondly recall taking them to see Somerset House at The Strand which Jane had mentioned in one of her letters. I also took them to Portobello Road market where they bought me an ornate French mirror from the 1790s. These were vibrant times, it was like springtime had returned to our lives. My quest for Jane was also the means of giving me a last few unforgettable golden days with my husband, Joe. He was not at all interested in Jane Austen's work, but he loved the sea and gladly accompanied me to many of the resorts she had brought to life in her novels. We took a railway trip to Lyme in Dorset to see the famous harbour wall, better known as the "Cobb", which Anne Elliot, and Captain Wentworth's party had walked along in *Persuasion*. It was near high tide and the waves were crashing up the harbour wall. I froze in fear at the thought that I could not swim and didn't venture another step. But Joe, so happy to be by the sea, strode off along its winding stones without a care. I was annoyed at the thought I wasn't going to walk the Cobb after all!

Another time we visited Bath arriving amid a lively and colourful fair. After taking a walk around the Roman baths we went on to see the Pump Room, the large elegant 18th century meeting place where Mrs Allen and Catherine had 'paraded up and down for an hour, looking at everybody and speaking to no one'. (*Northanger Abbey* p 25). I was anxious to move on to the Bath Assembly Rooms, one of the premier venues for concerts, parties and balls in Jane Austen's time. By now Joe was more interested in having "a pint". So we parted, Joe finding a nice inn as I went off to explore at my leisure. My plan to see the Assembly Rooms was briefly curtailed at the front door by a good looking, impeccably dressed, young waiter carrying a 'silver tray'. Looking at me sternly he said "Madam you cannot enter here". I replied asking if I could see the Ballroom just for a moment. "Sorry, you cannot" he scoffed and walked off. I was in a state of disbelief but I knew I just had to get inside to have a look. Facing me, covering the entrance across the hallway were the most beautiful deep red velvet drapes. I spotted an opening in them, and on impulse, quietly and quickly stepped through. I found myself in a most beautifully dressed room, pristine and classy, with sparkling chandeliers and gilded decor. I briefly rested on a luxurious chair enjoying the thought that this was one of the rooms that Jane had brought us to in her fiction. Then, happy with my little rebellious adventure, I got up and walked back out into the sunlight. I returned to the inn to see Joe sitting outside enjoying a pint of Guinness which he declared was the best he had tasted in his life.

Some time later my brother John, a parish Priest in Bishops Waltham, took Bernadette and myself on a day trip to nearby 'Chawton Cottage', the pretty little house where Jane had lived for the last eight years of her life. At the entrance, we bought an information booklet and were shown into a room with a long table running down the centre. I spotted a white china tea set and rushed over impulsively taking up one of the cups in my hand. As I admired the gold and navy rim, I saw, from the corner of my eye, a woman hurrying towards me. She had an amused but kind look on her face as she gently put her hand under the cup I held to save it from its possible demise. I apologised for my eagerness but she put me at ease right away. We continued on and I saw the Topaz crosses given to Jane and Cassandra by their brother Charles after he returned home from sea. A real event which Jane mimics in *Mansfield Park* where William, a midshipman, gives a Topaz cross to his sister Fanny. Before leaving I ran my hand along the writing desk given to Jane by her father on her nineteenth birthday. Finally, displayed on a wall in the narrow hallway, I came across a prayer written by Jane revealing her deep spirituality and compassion.

"Incline us to think humbly of ourselves, to be severe only in the examination of our own conduct, to consider our fellow creatures with kindness, and to judge of all they say and do with that charity, which we would desire from them ourselves."

The more I learnt about Jane the more I became aware of references and citations to Ireland in her novels. Up to now I had read Jane's novels, and other literature about her, for pure pleasure. But the Irish connections forced a subtle change from reading to investigation. As I researched, three names continually cropped up and so caught my attention. I had heard little, if anything, about them before, but was fascinated to find that all three had associations with Ireland. The first was Irish born playwright, and British politician, Richard Sheridan. The second was Maria Edgeworth, a renowned 'Irish' writer. Finally, there was Tom Lefroy who Jane had loved and lost during the Christmas season of 1795. I would later go on to discover the huge influence that both Richard Sheridan and Maria Edgeworth had on Jane's writing. At that time, however I was content just to have discovered these new authors whose writing I enjoyed nearly as much as Jane's.

The actual idea of writing a book came one happy summer evening in 1998 during a walk, in Covent Garden with John and our friend Ursula. They asked about my interest in Jane's novels and I started telling them about the references to Ireland that I had started to document. It was the first time I had shared this knowledge with others and it felt good. My brother looked at me quizzically, but I recall Ursula, herself a Jane Austen admirer, enthusiastically agreeing with me that "Ireland is indeed mentioned in *Emma*". I continued to confer the Irish links that I had found and I could see they had become engrossed. By the end of the evening, in the glow of their encouragement, I had talked myself into writing a book.

As his superb plays, his association with Drury Lane Theatre and his enthralling life so astonished and intrigued me, I chose to attempt my first chapter on Richard Sheridan. I started writing with pen and paper but later, in a Women's Welfare shop, I found an old electronic word processor that saved to tapes going for a 'fiver' that I thought I could use. The kind women running the shop personally delivered it to my home and even set it up for me. I finished the first draft of the Sheridan chapter on that machine, I still have the tapes to this day. I posted the final draft to Ursula for review. She returned it to me with written comments stating that it was a list of Sheridan's Plays but she could see no evidence of connections to Jane Austen. I was a little startled at her comments and began to question if I had the proficiency to write this, or any, book. I had researched both writers for some years and had amassed a mountain of notes but I had failed to convey anything of consequence in writing. At that time, I was a long way from unearthing the true nature of Sheridan's influence on Jane's works and life, but a knowing intuition sent me back to scrutinizing his plays and her novels once again.

Serendipity soon intervened. I had a friend who was accustomed to bringing me editions of the newspaper, *The Cork Examiner,* and in one edition I gazed in wonderment as I read;

"Unique Cork silver up for auction.

Between seven and ten thousand pounds is expected at a Sotheby sale on July 24th for a very rare 22 carat gold freedom box engraved with the coat of arms of the City of Cork. The box was presented at Cork in 1795 to the Lord Lieutenant of Ireland, William Fitzwilliam."

1795! William Fitzwilliam! in a flash of insight I knew that there was a connection between William Fitzwilliam and Jane Austen's hero of *Pride and Prejudice,* Fitzwilliam Darcy. I felt as if I had unearthed Tutankhamun's Tomb. A new world opened up for me as I searched for evidence to support my idea. I phoned Bernadette to tell her of my 'discovery' and her enthusiasm matched my own. During my next visit to Cork, Bernadette and myself excitedly set off for The Mansion House, the beautiful eighteenth century mayoral residence where "Mr. Darcy" had been given the gold freedom box.

We felt regal as we walked up its elegant staircase admiring the Georgian paintings. The house is situated by a tranquil part of the river Lee where swans and waterfowl shelter in its leafy banks. Later we sat there, chatting, gleefully imagining the Cork of 1795.

I became captivated with the life of the 4th Earl Fitzwilliam. He was one of the wealthiest men in England and yet, unusually for the sort, was frequently described as a "good man". I read of his ancestors, the Fitzwilliams and Darcys and visited some of their graves near the Aldwych in London. The 4th Earl Fitzwilliam was further connected to names like Watson, Wentworth and Woodhouse which also appeared in Jane's fiction. A new facet to Jane's personality was being revealed. The Fitzwilliam link led me deeper into the history of Ireland and I was soon thrown from the world of Jane Austen into the sad history of my own country's indomitable past. It was hard not to be affected. I thought it a tragedy for Ireland that Fitzwilliam was recalled to Westminster in 1795 as he was perhaps the only one who could have prevented the 1798 rebellion.

I started actually writing this book during the summer of 1998 but the months that followed would conspire to drag me from the world of Jane and her Irish connections. That December my husband asked me about the book for the first time. I assured him that I would complete it one day and he would be proud of me. He died a few days later. Shortly after, my sisters Margaret and Bernadette, who had so lovingly accompanied me on many of my 'Austen' excursions, were also taken by cancer. I had also begun treatment for cancer myself. Life had changed suddenly and drastically and I no longer had the enthusiasm to write. "The Book", as it had become affectionately known within the family, was set aside.

Over the following years I regularly talked about getting back to the book but never did. Friends and family continued to encourage me. My brother John regularly sent me articles he had found about Jane, and I kept a sort of nagging dialogue with myself about my failure to write. I recall my son Paul saying, "Mom, everyone knows about the book you're not writing".

Later, while on holiday in Cork, my sister Theresa and I took a trip to Cove, the main maritime town in Cork Harbour. The day yielded a delightful surprise view over the harbour which evoked many happy memories for me. The knowledge that Charles and Frank Austen's ships would have been regularly moored there in the harbour rekindled my interest in Jane and the book. Before leaving for London, as I knew that Jane had loved Maria Edgeworth's writing, I also fulfilled a wish to visit Maria's home in Co. Longford. The bug for Jane had got me again and a few days later in London I visited Sheridan's Drury Lane theatre with a good friend of mine. The experience was an inspiration. That evening, as I sat at my table with Sheridan's plays and Jane's novels, the illumination which I had yearned for so much came at last.

While reading a first draft of this chapter my son commented that it was more a diary of day trips rather than an introductory chapter. The text has since been much edited but I was, and still am, trying to convey that it was the visits that inspired me to write. It was the visits that sent me on an exhilarating journey of discovery and enlightenment. From Bath, the Hampshire Downs, and London, through the centuries back to my own Irish homeland, Jane Austen brought me on the journey of a lifetime and the story of that journey is the essence of this book.

CHAPTER 2

IRELAND AND MY WILD IRISH GIRL

Jane never crossed the Irish Sea, and never allowed any of her fictional characters to go to Ireland. They would be in 'danger of giving false representations' as she advised her niece Anna who was writing her own book in the summer of 1814. (Lt 98).

Jane wrote her novels between 1793 and 1816 a time of crisis all over Europe. It was the era of sailing ships which reached its zenith near the close of the 18th Century. England was continually at war with France, who was now in the shadow of The French Revolution and England was also beginning to have trouble ruling her western neighbour Ireland. Twelve percent of the officers, and up to 60% of ordinary seamen were Irish, serving and fighting alongside the English in battle (Barthelemy). However, in the latter half of the 1790s, Ireland had begun to have rapidly escalating rebellions and mutinies of its Irish sailors serving in the English Fleet.

The Romantic Movement swept across Europe in the late 18th and early 19th Centuries, and had a profound effect on art, literature and music. The popular view of Ireland was that of a country of legend and myth with a rich culture of crafts, storytelling, poetry, performance and music. The leisured classes were eager to learn about Ireland's ancient times, its castles, its illuminated manuscripts and the 'living traditions' of its Gaelic speaking areas. There was also the fascination of a country which had never been fully subdued by the English despite its continual endeavour to do so. This "Romantic" view was in stark contrast with the realities of Ireland of the time. English economic interest, anti-Catholic prejudice and harsh legislation kept the majority of the Irish in political suppression and devastating poverty.

The Austens of Hampshire hailed from gentry and had aristocratic ancestry on their mother's side. The family of five boys and two girls were without wealth or inheritance but had talent and drive enough to succeed in the world. The family environment and events of the time, much involving Ireland, were prime material for Jane's blossoming writing. Several of Jane's letters to Cassandra have survived and tell us of important events in the lives of Jane's two young adventurous brothers who chose careers in the navy. Frank, born in 1774, entered the Royal Naval Academy, Portsmouth, in 1786. Two years later he became a midshipman on the *Perseverance* which sailed for the East Indies in December 1788. He was 14 years old and his father wrote him a long letter of advice which he kept all his life. His father reminded him of his place in society, and though he may have little "dealings" with his "inferiors, when it does occur there is a sort of kindness they have a claim on you for, and which, you may believe me, will not be thrown away on them". Younger brother Charles was born in 1779 and in 1791 also joined the Royal Naval Academy.

Mansfield Park and *Persuasion*.

Jane, who was born in 1775, began to write her *Juvenilia* in her teens and in a wonderful expression of sisterly love, devoted much of her writing between 1789 and 1793 to her sailor brothers. She dedicated *Jack and Alice* (*MW* pp 12/29) and a 'tale' *Mr Harley* (*MW* p 40) to Frank while he served on the *Perseverance*. She also dedicated two very short tales, *Sir William Montague* (*MW* pp 40/42). and *Memoirs of Mr Clifford* (*MW* pp 43/44) to Charles. Twenty years later we can discern her life-long affection for them in the portraits of the naval characters in *Mansfield Park* and *Persuasion*.

A link can be made between Frank Austen and the Irish troubles as he was 'cruising' on the *Seahorse* around home waters in late 1796 and 1797. Cruising was then used as a euphemistic concealment for the act of spying or a deliberate show of force with the purpose of protecting British interests. After the Society of United Irishmen was outlawed and some of its greatest leaders executed, Ireland began to seek military help from France. One of the Society's founders, Wolfe Tone, a 28-year-old Protestant barrister who had published a pamphlet stressing the hope of substituting "the common name Irishmen" in place of "Protestant, Catholic and Dissenter" was ordered to leave for America. Instead he immediately set sail for France intending to get military help. In such revolutionary times the maverick Wolfe Tone was viewed as a figure of fear by the English establishment rather than one of justice let alone romance and idealism. In 1796 he published a further pamphlet, An Address to The People of Ireland On the Present Important Crisis – He wrote that many of the English fleet's crews would be ready to mutiny.

"Who are they that man their vessels? Two Thirds of them are Irishmen; and will those brave and gallant fellows, thousands of whom have been pressed, and the rest driven by famine into her service...be ready to turn their arms against their native land, against their fathers, their brothers, their wives, their children, and their friends?"

In December 1796, a French expedition of forty-five ships and 14,750 men, Wolfe Tone among them, set sail from Brest, on the west coast of France, to Bantry Bay, Cork. They managed to sail right under the noses of the English Fleet, including Frank Austen's ship, but this epic attempt began, and ended in disaster. One ship sank in the channel coming out of Brest and another was lost in the raging seas around Cork. Due to the atrocious weather that greeted them they were prevented from landing and the invasion was finally abandoned. The French fleet returned home with the English none the wiser for some time after.

The following year in May 1797, at the Nore near Sheerness in Kent, Irish sailors serving in the English Fleet staged a mutiny. Their euphoria was short lived, as the mutiny was soon crushed by the ferocious Admiral Jervis. An eyewitness account tells - "After the Mutinies at the Nore in 1797 the *Seahorse* sent a boat to attend punishments round the fleet." Frank Austen was twenty-four at the time and was serving on the *Seahorse*. Many of the ships were ordered to Cadiz and in September Frank Austen would have witnessed the floggings and hangings there. In the log of *The London*, one of the ships of the line blockading Cadiz, six executions are recorded as taking place among the ships of the fleet off Cadiz. "The *Marleborough* was anchored in the middle of the line. At 7 O'clock she made the signs for punishment. The London sent out launch, barge and cutter - At 9 O'clock, Peter Anderson of the *Marleborough* was put to death for mutiny." Frank Austen at a young age experienced the cruelty and violence of life at sea. Yet if the crews of his ships were up to 60% Irish he would have come to learn much about their character especially their love of freedom and fairness. How much he told Jane of the Nore mutiny is not known. Decades later, in the 1840s, during the time of the great famine, Frank made a contribution to a charity for the 'Irish Poor'.

In June 1798, without leadership or French help, the Irish rose up in Rebellion. In Wexford, there was a moment of glory when Wexford town and its surroundings were hailed a republic, while at Wexford harbour Captain Williams, who had married Jane Austen's first cousin was taking prisoners on board his ship the *Endymion*. Later in the month of August, the French landed in Co. Mayo but were defeated by the English army at Ballinamuck Co. Longford. In October, the French Fleet arrived off the coast of Donegal in a raging storm and the English Fleet were waiting for them. Wolfe Tone was on board the flagship *Hoche* and the French officers wanted him to escape back to France in a fast sailing frigate, but he was said to have replied 'Shall it be said of me that I fled whilst the French were fighting the battles of my country?'. He was captured and taken to Dublin. Sentenced to be hanged, he died after cutting his own throat in November 1798. The English had got their man, but his principles and ideals were the firm conviction "to subvert the tyranny of our execrable government, to break the connection with England…to assert the independence of my country" (WT address). It is estimated that over 30,000 people died in the 1798 Rebellion, more than in the entire terror of The French Revolution. Aislings were no longer written in the hope of a Stuart king returning but the heroes of 1798 are remembered in the poetry and song of Ireland.

"Romantic Ireland's dead and gone,
It's with O'Leary in the grave,
Yet they were of a different kind,
The names that stilled your childish play,
They have gone about the world like wind,

But little time had they to pray,
For whom the hangman's rope was spun,
And what, God help us, could they save?
Romantic Ireland's dead and gone,
It's with O'Leary in the grave.
Was it for this the Wild Geese spread,
The grey wing upon every tide;
For this that all that blood was shed.
For this Edward Fitzgerald died,
And Robert Emmet and Wolfe Tone.
All that delirium of the brave?
Romantic Ireland's dead and gone,
It's with O'Leary in the grave."
WB Yates (1913)

Jane started writing her novels in 1793 just as her other brother Henry joined the Oxfordshire Militia. He was sent to Ireland in 1799 where his duty was primarily to guard against a French Invasion. Although no letters to Jane survive from his posting it is highly likely that Henry would have told Jane tales of Ireland and Irish officers giving her material for her first three novels. *Sense and Sensibility* has a Colonel Brandon, *Northanger Abbey* has a Captain Tilney, and *Pride and Prejudice* has Colonel Forster, Mr Wickham and the officers. Around the year 1803 Jane began to write *The Watsons* and one of its characters, a Mr Edwards, refers to Ireland in a dubious way. "Irish! Ah! I remember - and she is gone to settle in Ireland. - I do not wonder that you should not wish to go with her into that Country Miss Emma". When Emma tells him that her widowed aunt has now married a Captain O'Brien he declares. "There is nothing like your officers for captivating the Ladies, Young or Old - There is no resisting a Cockade my dear" (*MW* pp 326).

About ten years later in her novel *Mansfield Park*, after Frank and Charles would have been at sea for over 24 years, Jane writes this phrase; "If any one faculty of our nature may be called more wonderful than the rest, I do think it is memory" (*MP* p 208). In the novel, it appears that Jane herself takes a wistful trip down memory lane to the time of her youth when her brothers began sailing the high seas. She takes ten-year-old Fanny Price from a poor home in Portsmouth to live with her rich cousins, the Bertrams, at *Mansfield*

Park. As the cousins discuss Fanny's education with their Aunt Norris, one sister comments "But, aunt...we asked her last night, which way she would go to get to Ireland; and she said she should cross to the Isle of Wight" (*MP* p18). There is a specific link here with Jane's own life when at a similar age to Fanny she did go to Portsmouth with her family in 1786, on twelve-year-old Frank entering the Royal Naval Academy.

The naval experiences and exploits of Jane's brothers are further reflected in her novels with such details as William Price telling his sister Fanny that, "The Portsmouth girls turn up their noses at anybody who has not a commission. One might as well be nothing as a midshipman" (*MP* p 249) and Fanny consoles him that "it is no more than what the greatest admirals have all experienced" (*MP* p 249). Later there is great rejoicing when William is made a Lieutenant. In further Portsmouth scenes, Jane gives details of the Thrush in "a cruise to the Westward" leaving the "sally-port' for Spithead encapsulating the experiences of her brothers' departure to patrol the Irish waters.

In *Mansfield Park*, young William can be identified as the aspiring naval hero living the romantic life at sea but in *Persuasion* Jane preserves the necessity of rank with the role of the disciplined Admiral Croft and Captains Wentworth, Harville, and Benwick. Yet in their personal lives they are free to determine their own chosen paths.

In *Persuasion*, which she was writing around the year 1816, Jane has Louisa Musgrove 'burst forth into raptures of admiration and delight on the character of the navy - their friendliness, their brotherliness, their openness, their uprightness...convinced of sailors having more worth and warmth than any other set of men in England; that they only knew how to live, and they only deserved to be respected and loved' (*PER* p 99).

The nobility of England and Ireland.

Many of the characters in Jane Austen's novels had the names of her ancestors, who had played noted roles in the making of England and Ireland over the centuries. It seems they were always a focal point in her thought.

Interest in her own family history is obvious, as Elliot, one of the names of her ancestors, appears in *Persuasion*. Here, Sir Walter Elliot of Kellynch Hall, frequently takes up the *Baronetage*, a history of his ancestors, reading 'with an interest which never failed' (*PER* p 3). One morning, Sir Walter Elliot reads in the newspaper that his cousins, 'the Dowager Viscountess Dalrymple, and her daughter', were coming to Bath 'and the agony was, how to introduce themselves properly' (*PER* p 148).

Sir Walter's daughter, Anne, declines a further visit to the Dalrymples saying that she had arranged to visit her friend, Mrs Smith. Sir Walter then snaps back, "an every day Mrs. Smith...to be the chosen friend of Miss Anne Elliot, and to be preferred by her, to her own family connections among the nobility of England and Ireland!" (*PER* p 158).

The nobility of England and Ireland is linked because of its shared roots in the Norman conquest and the title of the Dalrymples is an old one which must be respected. To the vain and snobbish Sir Walter Elliot, a name invokes bloodline, ancestry, lineage and such a name as Smith means nothing to him but it does to Anne, who has come to know Mrs Smith. Some time later, Sir Walter preserves the distinction of rank again. He and his daughters arrive early to an evening concert and take 'their station' by one of the fires in the Octagon room to await Lady Dalrymple who 'must be waited for' (*PER* p 181).

Jane's personal voice in *Persuasion*

During the concert, as the Elliots and the Dalrymples were listening to an Italian love song, Lady Dalrymple sees Captain Wentworth. She remarks on his appearance to Sir Walter, saying "A very fine young man indeed! ...More air than one often sees in Bath - Irish I dare say" (*PER* p 188). Captain Wentworth is English but, because of his bearing, Lady Dalrymple assumes he could be Irish. Was this Jane Austen's personal voice associating 'a very fine young man' with Irishman, Tom Lefroy, whom she had known twenty years earlier? In her last novel, she could look back and perhaps feel a little affection for a man who went away and never contacted her again. Her sorrowful comment to Captain Harville is revealing "All the privilege I claim for my own sex...is that of loving longest, when existence or when hope is gone" (*PER* p 235).

Jane Austen, King Charles I, and Ireland

Another connection between Ireland and Jane is the Stuart king Charles I. The Irish had a short relief in the 17th Century under Charles I who came to the throne in 1625. They loved this Stuart king and it seems Jane Austen and her family reflected a similar homage to him. Jane's ancestors on her mother's side, the Leighs, were fervently loyal to Charles I, and when the Mayor and Magistrates of Coventry slammed their gates against him, Sir Thomas Leigh welcomed the king into his home. Charles I repaid Sir Thomas for his loyalty by creating him Baron Leigh of Stoneleigh in July 1643, but the Cromwellian government demanded £4895 from him to keep his estates. Jane wrote her short comic, *History of England*, when she was fifteen and declares that Charles I 'suffered misfortunes equal to those of his lovely grandmother' (*MW* p 148), Mary Queen of Scots. She writes of 'vindicating him from the...tyrannical Government...with one argument...that he was a STUART' (*MW* pp 149/150). One of her 'leaders of the Gang' of Villains, of her 'tyrannical Government' was Oliver Cromwell himself, who came to Ireland in 1649 and inflicted tyranny on the Irish Catholics. In the same year, Charles I was beheaded and was greatly mourned by them. Their bards began to write Aislings, poems in Gaelic, where Ireland is depicted as a beautiful woman hoping for the return of her lover, a Stuart King.

Ireland mentioned in her letters

Jane mentions Ireland in her letters, commenting in a casual way as if she knew the place. She writes to Cassandra in 1808 that their nephew, Edward, was reading "*The Lake of Killarney*, twisting himself about in one of our great chairs" (Lt 59). To Frank, in July 1813, she writes "Our Cousins Colonel Thomas Austen & Margaretta are going Aid-de-camps to Ireland & Lord Whitworth goes in their train as Lord Lieutenant...We join in an infinity of love" (Lt 81). And to Cassandra again in 1813 "I have...such sweet flattery from Miss Sharp!...I am read and admired in Ireland too" (Lt 90).

The Wild Irish Girl (1806) and the ambiguity of *Emma* (1816)

Reading one of Jane's letters, I made another discovery that she had read Miss Sidney Owenson's *The Wild Irish Girl* (1806) and did not like it. However, after reading this novel myself I saw clearly that she used it as a template for characters and situations in her intriguing *Emma*.

Of her six novels, *Emma,* has the most references to Ireland. Jane wrote to Cassandra in January 1809 that she was reading *Ida of Athens* "We have only read the Preface yet; but her Irish Girl does not make me expect much - if the warmth of her language could affect the Body it might be worth reading in this weather" (Lt 64). Jane's sarcastic remark is perhaps justifiable, as the Irish author Miss Sidney Owenson's romantic novel was hugely successful, while her own work was, as yet, unpublished. Crucially, it can also be gleaned from the novel that Owenson disliked and criticised the Stuarts and Jane would not have taken kindly to this.

In *The Wild Irish Girl,* Owenson's writing epitomises the Romantic era. Its tendency to sentimental, over blown, metaphysical excesses of language contrasts forcibly with Jane Austen's restrained and witty writing, where a 'small sort of societal morality' is cultivated.

Owenson demonstrates her Romantic appreciation of the Irish landscape; "We now continued to proceed through a country, rich in all the boundless extravagance of picturesque beauty, where Nature's sublimest features everywhere present themselves, carelessly disposed in wild magnificence...The far-stretched ocean, mountains of alpine magnitude, heaths of boundless desolation, vales of romantic loveliness, navigable rivers, and extensive lakes...while the ruins of an ancient castle, or the mouldering remains of a desolated abbey...the pleasure derived from the contemplation of Nature in her happiest and most varied aspect"(*TWIG* p 191). Owenson is describing the scenic beauty of the West of Ireland, which could be Connemara.

Whereas Jane Austen describes an English country scene in *Emma*;

"It was hot; and after walking...over the gardens in a scattered, dispersed way...they...followed one another to the delicious shade of a broad short avenue of limes, which stretching beyond the garden at an equal distance from the river, seemed the finish of the pleasure grounds - It led to nothing...but a view...over a low stone wall...intended...to give the appearance of an approach to the house...it was...extremely pretty...the foot of which the Abbey stood...was a bank of considerable abruptness and grandeur...and at the bottom of this bank...rose the Abbey-Mill Farm, with meadows in front, and the river making a... handsome curve around it. It was a sweet view - sweet, to the eye and the mind. English verdure, English culture, English comfort, seen under a sun bright, without being oppressive" (*E* p 360).

In *The Wild Irish Girl*, Miss Owenson is vigorously intent on promoting her political, economic, and social message about conditions in Ireland because of English policy. Her romantic novel with its epic tragic pretensions is a vehicle to get across this message expressed and exhibited through her characters. The hero of the novel is Horatio Mortimer who is banished to his father's estate in the West of Ireland 'a country against which I have a decided prejudice...which I suppose semi-barbarous, semi-civilized' (*TWIG* p 10). He anguishes about his role as 'hereditary object of hereditary detestation' and the part his family have played in the economic and cultural repression of Ireland.

He is the storyteller and he depicts how the characters are seen, chiefly Glorvina, the Princess of Inishmore, whose character is used as a cipher to spread knowledge and sentimental romanticising of Irish culture.

Horatio falls in love with Glorvina and describes her in a poetic style of language. "She started and turned round, and in surprise let fall her flowers, yet she smiled, and seemed confused - but pleasure, pure animated life-breathing pleasure, was the predominant expression of her countenance. The Deity of Health was never personified in more glowing colours - her eyes rich blue, her cheeks crimson blush, her lips dewy freshness, the wanton wildness of her golden tresses, the delicious languor that mellowed the fire of her beamy glance - I gazed, and worshipped' (*TWIG* p 140). Glorvina is a true romantic heroine, close to nature but very well read and intelligent. She is perfectly selfless and willing to sacrifice herself to help her father and her country. She speaks several languages, sings beautifully, and plays the Harp exquisitely.

In *Emma*, Jane Austen models her Jane Fairfax on Glorvina, echoing her excellence in accomplishments and looks. She describes Jane's beauty, 'Her height, was pretty...her figure particularly graceful... Her eyes, a deep grey, with dark eyelashes and eyebrows...the skin...had a clearness and delicacy which really needed no fuller bloom. It was a style of beauty, of which elegance was the reigning character' (*E* p 167). Like Glorvina, Jane Fairfax too, is modest and well read. Not only has she superiority both in beauty and acquirements' (*E* p 165) but is also a 'mistress of music' (*E* p 215) and has a beautiful voice and sings in Italian.

Although Miss Owenson promotes her Glorvina as an ideal of Romantic womanhood, Jane Austen is sceptical indicating her dislike of such "pictures of perfection" (Lt 142) and her Jane Fairfax is sent up and disliked for her accomplishments, admirable but not likeable. Jane Austen is not interested in the social message and crusade of Owenson and in *Emma* makes fun of Gothic Romanticism, using 'Romantic' Ireland as a source of humour. Here she betrays an ascendency viewpoint. Also, Jane Fairfax is secretly engaged to Frank Churchill and they practise deception to conceal their romance.

We share Emma's irritation when faced with Jane Fairfax's much praised accomplishments. Jane Fairfax is shown as a 'man's woman' and even the perceptive Mr Knightley is susceptible to her charms. Emma confesses that she 'was prone to take disgust towards a girl so idolized and so cried up' (*E* p 203). It is obviously infuriating for Emma that Jane Fairfax inspires chivalry and attracts the Romantic Hero. Jane Austen sets Jane Fairfax up as the archetypal romantic heroine who needs to be rescued like Glorvina but injects fun into the process. Emma is frustrated that this creature can have such power over men. By contrast, Emma herself has prejudices and is vain, and shows an attitude of superiority to what she thinks are Jane Fairfax's feminine wiles. Yet she is supremely human and envies Jane Fairfax who is the successful romantic heroine.

Miss Owenson's writing is steeped in the Romantic excesses of the age. Jane Austen is also part of this romanticism and, though she treats it with scepticism, she does not dismiss it. She shows how Emma deals with the complications of her social world, and Jane Fairfax is a part of the process. At the same time, Jane Austen creates a happy romantic ending for both Emma and Jane Fairfax.

She also offers the view that such surface perfection in Jane Fairfax may hide her true character. Could she be scheming for a rich marriage, or is she simply a woman in love, a victim of her lover's plotting? She appears as a sort of romantic fashion victim, both exploited and exploiting. Frank Churchill has the dashing attributes of the classic hero but his actions and motives are not so pure. Mr Dixon, already married in Ireland was wrongly seen as the admirer of Jane Fairfax. Frank encourages this error to distract from his own secret engagement to her. He deliberately deceives Emma when he tells her "here are a new set of Irish melodies. That, from such a quarter, one might expect" (*E* p 242).

The high Romanticism of Horatio's rescue of Glorvina (*TWIG* p 248) contrasts with the actions of Mr Dixon, as Miss Bates fuels Emma's fanciful imagination in telling how Mr Dixon saved Jane Fairfax from drowning. Jane Austen's amusing narration pays tribute to 'the cult of the Heroic' with its celebration of the "frisson" of danger with this rescue. "Ever since the service he rendered Jane at Weymouth, when they were out in that party on the water, and she, by the sudden whirling round of…the sails, would have be dashed into the sea…if he had not…caught hold of her habit - (I can never think of it without trembling!)" (*E* p 160/1).

In *Emma*, Mr Dixon has married the Campbells' daughter and taken her to live in Ireland at his 'country seat Balycraig' (*E* p 159). Bally is an ancient Gaelic word for town and Craig suggests a rocky, rough or mountainous place. It is possible Jane might have created her own 'Balycraig' on reading of the 109-year-old legendary harpist Dennis Hampson, 'a native of Craigmore…County Derry' (*TWIG* p 200, notes).

The image of Ireland as a land of plenty is given emphasis when Emma discusses with Frank Churchill the reason for Jane Fairfax "choosing to come to Highbury instead of going with the Campbells to Ireland. Here she must be leading a life of privation and penance; there it would have been all enjoyment" (*E* p 217). The comparison between the less pleasant conditions which Jane Fairfax must endure in Highbury because of her love for Frank Churchill emphasises the Dixons richer and pleasanter lifestyle in Ireland. It also reflects the reputation of the Ascendancy for ostentatious living as opposed to their more reserved "British" parallels. Jane could also be adopting the attitude that Ireland was a land of plenty, which was a source of admiration as well as envy and criticism.

This bias concerning Irish flamboyance is reinforced by Frank's remarks about Jane Fairfax's hairstyle, "but really Miss Fairfax has done her hair in so odd a way...that I cannot keep my eyes from her...Those curls! I must go and ask her whether it is an Irish fashion" (*E* p 222). Jane Austen is making fun of Miss Owenson's detailed description of the traditional way the Irish once wore their hair. Jane Austen by using 'Irish fashion' in this somewhat unfavourable way reveals a viewpoint of Ireland as an object of humour and mockery. Ireland is made a focal point again for Frank's cunning bluff and deception, involving both humour and arrogance, while Frank himself is flirting and using Irish references, to help deflect attention, and disguise his deceit.

When Emma remarks 'as to the expedition and the expense of the Irish Mails' (*E* p 298) Jane Austen could be referring to its cost or commenting on the expansive language of Miss Owenson, who has Horatio describe the service in vivid, glowing terms, "As we had the mail on board, a boat was sent out to receive it, the oars of which were plied by six men, whose statues, limbs, and features, declared them the lingering progeny of the once formidable race of Irish giants...which might have individually afforded a model to sculpture, for the colossal statue of an Hercules...as they stemmed the mountainous waves, or plied their heavy oars" (*TWIG* p 14).

One Kingdom but different countries

Jane Austen's attitude to 'that country' Ireland, might be discerned in what she has the character of Miss Bates say in *Emma*. Miss Bates who is pivotal to the plot and always tells the truth declares, "the Campbells are going to Ireland. Mrs Dixon has persuaded her father and mother to come over and see her...which must make it very strange to be in different kingdoms, I was going to say, but however different countries" (*E* p 159). Miss Bates has the knack of making an important error only to correct it instantly. In 1801 Ireland and England became one Kingdom under the reign of George III but as Jane Austen perceived in the words of Miss Bates, they remained very "different countries".

I believe that Jane Austen's perception of Gaelic Ireland, its history and culture might have been re-evaluated after she read *The Wild Irish Girl*.

Lord Nelson and Captain Austen...an excellent young man

Jane wrote to Cassandra in October 1813 of a book just published, and says "Southey's Life of Nelson; I am tired of Lives of Nelson being that I never read any. I will read this however, if Frank is mentioned in it" (Lt 86). Frank Austen had long associations with Lord Nelson. In 1797 he was Senior Lieutenant on the *Seahorse* which took Lord Nelson to England. In 1798 as Commander of the *Peterel*, Nelson thanked him personally at Palermo on delivery of an important dispatch. In 1805 the year of Trafalgar, Frank's ship the *Leopard* joined the Mediterranean fleet and Nelson commended that "Captain Austen…an excellent young man" be transferred to the *Canopus*. This ship followed Lord Nelson's fleet across the Atlantic in the chase to find the French Fleet. Managing to escape capture the French Fleet return to Cadiz. Lord Nelson and his fleet now blockaded Cadiz. In September Frank and the *Canopus* was sent to Tetuan and Gibraltar for water and provisions, and in October Nelson seized his opportunity to draw the French and Spanish fleets out into the Atlantic and to their dire fate at the Battle of Trafalgar. Frank was destined not to take part. Part of Lord Nelson's prayer, written just before the battle reads "May the great God, whom I worship, grant to my Country and for the benefit of Europe in general, a great and glorious Victory: and may no misconduct, in any one, tarnish it and may humanity after victory be the predominant feature in the British Fleet".

Such omissions of the victories of Nelson and the British Fleet in Jane's novels are a reflection on her insistence on the personal and particular in her writing which was always inspired by her family environment. Undoubtedly Ireland did not impinge personally on Jane's experience, but was pivotal in her brothers' early naval experiences and as such impacted directly on Jane's consciousness and writing.

CHAPTER 3

LORD EDWARD FITZGERALD

An opportunity came from a family friend, for Bernadette, John and myself to stay at the gorgeous Georgian Glin House, in the village of Glin, Co. Limerick in early 2003. This was one of the wonderful trips of my life and our last trip together to one of the most beautiful places in the world. Soon we realised we were in the ancestral home of a branch of the great Norman family the Fitzgeralds or Geraldines, Earls of Desmond. I was delighted to be able to speak to one of this family's descendent who confirmed that Lord Edward Fitzgerald visited this house during the turbulent years of the 1790s. More historical detail in the fabric of Irish History during Jane Austen's time.

"The more free, the more Welcome" (*The Visit, MW* p 50)

The conversation between Miss Elizabeth Bennet and lady Catherine de Bourgh was critical and represented a turning point in *Pride and Prejudice*. Lady Catherine addresses Elizabeth referring to her as having "The upstart pretensions of a young woman without family, connections, or fortune...If you were sensible of your own good, you would not wish to quit the sphere, in which you have been brought up". Elizabeth, insulted replies "In marrying your nephew, I should not consider myself as quitting that sphere. He is a gentleman; I am a gentleman's daughter; so far we are equal" (p 356).

We find ourselves surprised maybe even astonished that a young lady at this time in history, and who hailed from gentry, should express such radical ideas as these. Where did Elizabeth get such ideas from? Where did Jane Austen get such ideas from?

Once again there was an Irish Connection. It all began in 1790 when Jane Austen as a young teenager wrote a short play, *The Visit* (*MW* pp 49-54), and it had a character named Lord Fitzgerald. At this time the leading aristocratic dynasty in Ireland were the Fitzgeralds of Kildare known as 'the premier peers' of Ireland. In the 1780s and 1790s the comings and goings of this glamorous family would have been reported in the newspapers frequently. The young Jane Austen is likely to have been fascinated by the size, eminence, and wealth of such a family and must have delighted in the romantic and slightly scandalous rumours and reports attaching to it.

In *The Visit*, Jane is using risqué Georgian humour in her daring social play which involves a shortage of chairs forcing certain characters to sit on others' laps. She is also using caricatures of known people, even contemporary celebrities. Lord Fitzgerald mentions that his Grandmother destroyed "the Hothouse in order to build a receptacle for the Turkeys" (*MW* p 54) and it is tantalising to speculate that the real Lord Edward Fitzgerald had sailed home from North America in 1789 and as it is well known at this time 'Turkeys' were becoming much more accepted as a popular fowl at the table, but imported from America originally.

Jane Austen may have picked the name Fitzgerald because Lord Edward Fitzgerald was a descendent of the Stuart King, Charles II and Jane liked the Stuarts. Charles and his French mistress, Louise de Keroualle, (given to him by the French king Louis XIV in 1670) had a son in 1672 and he was given the title of Duke of Richmond. In 1747 Lady Emily, the sixteen-year-old, daughter of the then Duke of Richmond married Lord Fitzgerald, Earl of Kildare, and went to live with him in Dublin, Ireland. Later they became the Duke and Duchess of Leinster. Of their nineteen children, nine survived to adulthood, four daughters and five sons. Lord Edward, born in 1763 was said to have been the brightest and most intelligent of the children and seems to have been his mother's favourite child.

His army life in America - and living with the Iroquois.

A lover of adventure, Lord Edward, having trained at a military academy in Paris, joined his uncle the Duke of Richmond's Militia, and was sent to America where his first assignment was tending prisoners during the war of Independence. One of the prisoners a Colonel Washington said of him "I never knew so lovable a person, and every man in the army, from the general to the drummer, would cheer the expression...his valour almost chivalrous...made him the idol of all who served with him" (*Citizen Lord* p 35).

Another assignment in America brought Lord Edward into contact with the Iroquois and he was eager for, and admired their way of life. They had a proud history. In 1570 an inspired Huron mystic Deganawidah, brought a message of hope and goodwill to the woodland tribes of upstate New York, urging them to stop arguing and form one brotherhood, which later became known to the Indians as the Great Peace and to the Europeans as the League of the Iroquois. They founded a colony at Quebec and traded around the St. Lawrence river, with the English and French. They kept the balance of power with their 'independent neutrality' and believed they were born free to go where they wished. They allowed into their lands "those who seem to us good" (*American Heritage* p 192).

At Detroit Lord Edward was honoured by the Seneca people and made a chieftain. He wrote to his mother that he had been adopted by one of the Nations and had become a 'thorough Indian' and kept the 'certificate' as evidence:

21st June 1789 - David Hill, Chief of the Six Nations, give the name of Eghnidal to my friend Lord Edward Fitzgerald, for which I hope he will remember me as long as he lives. The Name belongs to the Bear Tribe.

He wrote to his mother again from Lake Superior "I set out tomorrow. I have got a canoe...five men...a few presents for the Indian villages I pass through. Except for Indian corn and grease...I eat nothing else...it sounds bad, but it is not so...Few people know how little is necessary to live. What is called and thought hardship is nothing; one unhappy feeling is worse than a thousand years of it "(*Citizen Lord* p 108). This letter reveals a very idealistic Edward, finding peace far away from his opulent life back home.

He arrived back in England in late 1789 with his black servant Tony. He had been to the New World twice, travelled from the

Caribbean to Canada and found a little Utopia among the Iroquois. He remained in camp at Portsmouth with the 54th regiment until 1792. Lord Edward was an extremely charismatic personality and would have been well-known in army circles. The Austens and the Fitzgeralds may have crossed paths.

When Lord Edward returned from his assignments in America The French Revolution had taken place. It was an event that changed Europe even the World for ever; and its ideals of Liberty, Equality and Fraternity had entered the minds of people in many countries and allowed them to hope for more freedom and self-determination in their lives. In England, Reform, Radicalism and even Revolution were in the air, people wanted change. Thomas Paine wrote *The Rights of Man* which proposed a new social and political order. He was forced to leave England soon afterwards. Many leading members of *The London Corresponding Society, and The Society for Constitutional Information* were charged with High treason and imprisoned. One man, William Godwin, a political journalist who, in 1791, along with a friend wrote an open letter to Richard Sheridan 'advocating a revolution in Great Britain' (*A Traitor's Kiss* p 274), attacked the charge of High treason brought against these men and visited them in prison. He wrote a successful novel Caleb Williams about the evils of the then system of civilised society. He was also 'one of the radicals on a list of Paine's 'friends and acquaintance' topped by Lord Edward Fitzgerald' (*Citizen Lord*, p 11). So, Lord Edward Fitzgerald, William Godwin and Thomas Paine were three friends in a coterie of revolutionaries. In late 1792 Lord Edward Fitzgerald went to Paris to attend a conference held by Thomas Paine and shocked those present when he renounced his aristocratic title and choose to be known as 'le Citoyen Edouard Fitzgerald'. There was no turning back for him and he returned from Paris a revolutionary.

Jane Austen from 1792 onwards

Jane also used the name Fitzgerald several times in her short novel, *Lesley Castle* (*MW* pp 110/139, 1792). Between the years 1790 and 1796, from *The Visit* to her first draft of *Pride and Prejudice*, Jane like many young people began to want a more equal society and radical zeal entered her consciousness. I was soon convinced of this when in one of her letters it was obvious that she knew of William Godwin (Lt 37 May 1801 to Cassandra). She also would have read of

Lord Edward Fitzgerald's sensational behaviour in Paris. And she had read Thomas Paine's *The Rights of Man*. Immediately I solved my dilemma concerning Elizabeth Bennet's conversation with Lady Catherine de Bourgh in *Pride and Prejudice*. Eureka!

The encounter between Lady Catherine and Elizabeth Bennet takes place in "a prettyish kind of a little wilderness on one side of your lawn" (*PP* p 352). This is a metaphor for the 'garden of Eden' from Thomas Paine's book *The Rights of Man*. When Elizabeth, replies to lady Catherine "In marrying your nephew, I should not consider myself as quitting that sphere. He is a gentleman; I am a gentleman's daughter; so far we are equal" (p 356) again Jane has taken her quote from *The Rights of Man* where Thomas Paine wrote 'All men are born equal and with equal natural rights'.

In *Pride and Prejudice* Mr Darcy does not have a title, once more the influence of Thomas Paine's words is obvious, that 'there were no titles in the garden of Eden' and that 'society must now take the substantial ground of character, instead of the chimerical ground of titles'. Much later in the novel, when Elizabeth tells her mother that she and Mr Darcy are to be married, Mrs Bennet says of her future rich son-in-law "I can think of nothing else! Ten thousand a year...Tis as good as a Lord!" (p 378).

The master spy - Wickham - A name Jane Austen called her villain in *Pride and Prejudice*

It is a curious coincidence that Jane's villain in *Pride and Prejudice* is called George Wickham and he sets out to destroy Mr Darcy. I believe she had the master spy William Wickham in mind when she named her villain. William Wickham, had become the coordinator of Britain's spy network in 1793. The three radicals Fitzgerald, Paine and Godwin were known to this powerful man. His network of informers infiltrated the London Corresponding Society. In Ireland, his 'squalid network' of spies had penetrated the Society of United Irishmen at every level and a constant stream of information flowed towards Dublin Castle and then to London. In September, many of the leaders of the Society of United Irishmen of Ulster were arrested, and executed in Kilmainham gaol. Wickham left for Switzerland in October 1794 to build-up a substantive web of secret agents throughout Europe. A spy was planted in the midst of one supposedly 'safe haven' for United Irishmen in Hamburg, and

William Wickham targeted their mail. He was informed that coded information passed between members. Once again Jane Austen's narrative gives cause for reflection.

Lord Edward's Childhood - "My Dearest Mama...I long monstrously to see you"

Lord Edward's mother Lady Emily having read Rousseau's book *Emile de l'Education* wanted her children educated in the Rousseau ideal. In 1766 she purchased a villa near the sea at Blackrock, Co. Dublin called it Frescati, and it was here most of the Fitzgerald children were educated. Both boys and girls studied French, Classics and Maths together. Fencing, Deportment, going to the theatre and fishing trips were part of the curriculum; as was the care of cows and horses. Each child had their own patch of garden to cultivate. Lady Emily visited her children weekly and corresponded with each of them and continued this practice, especially with her sons thereafter. Lord Edward had a great love for his family and adored his mother writing to her frequently. As a youth in 1774 he wrote "My Dearest Mama, if I could go to see you, I would gallop away this very minute, I long monstrously to see you" (*Citizen Lord* p 19).

1792-1798 - Lord Edward marries, returns to Ireland and dies a revolutionary

In November 1792 after renouncing his title, he saw the beautiful Pamela de Genlis at the theatre in Paris, and married her some weeks later. He was twenty-nine and Pamela was nineteen and they signed their names 'citoyens' and 'citoyennes'. Pamela was the daughter of an aristocrat Madame de Genlis, who herself was a mistress of the future Duc d'Orleans. The newlyweds arrived in Dublin in January 1793, with Tony and their French maid Sophie and settled in Leinster House. In an Ireland dominated by a hard Ascendancy they were out of place, with their revolutionary clothes, and his cropped hair. He was criticized for walking the streets of Dublin rather than riding a horse.

He embraced Irish culture. His sister Lucy wrote "Dec.13th we had a dance in the evening our company was Cummins and the butcher's daughters...we danced a great many jigs. Ed is a great hand at them" (*Rebels and Informers* p 217). Soon he was disillusioned with Irish Politics 'Our Parliament did business yesterday...a new arrangement of revenues, a pension bill a place bill...no saving of expense, no abolition of places, and a great increase of taxes' (*Rebels and Informers* p 117). In early 1796 he spoke out against an insurrection Bill that proposed harsh punishments for several seditious activities and in May he took his family to Hamburg, a free port and Europe's spy capital.

Returns to his fate - becoming 'The People's Revolutionary'

In late 1796 Lord Edward returned to Ireland and joined the Society of United Irishmen. He became known as 'The People's Revolutionary' using his military expertise in training local units. He would walk the streets, attend country festivals, and sit in courtrooms to keep up his populism among the ordinary people. Organising for war became his life as he travelled throughout Ireland urging people to rise, even visiting his cousins at the Castle of Glin in County Limerick. Thomas Moore describes how he saw him walking down Grafton Street in 1797, and recalled thirty years later "on being told who he was...I ran anxiously after him, desirous of another look at one whose name had, from my schooldays, been associated in my mind with all that was noble, patriotic and chivalrous...the soft expression given to his eyes by their long dark lashes, are as present and familiar to my memory as if I had intimately known him" (*Fitzgerald's Life* by Thomas Moore).

In 1797, while staying at Frescati, he recalled to his mother of his pleasure in seeing the place again that he had "a thousand delightful feels about it...every peep of the house has a little history with it...The trees are all so grown that there are a thousand pretty sheltered spots, which near the sea...is very pleasant" (*Citizen Lord* p218-219). By now many of the Irish were desperate as the military were targeting villages and towns, and those in power sought revenge on individuals. By December 1797 Lord Edward was leading a secret life protected by a group of furtive men as he moved from place to place in his struggle to remain free.

His final months of disguise and secrecy

In March 1798, most of the leaders of the Society of United Irishmen were arrested, but Lord Edward was rushed through the stable yard of Leinster House by his faithful servant Tony and escaped. Lord Castlereagh offered huge rewards for his capture. In the final months of his life he took on mythical status as he went about Dublin in many different disguises. His loyalty was tested when his stepfather Mr Ogilvie met him in secret and told him of Lord Clare's offer of freedom 'the ports shall be thrown open to you, and no hindrance whatever offered' but Lord Edward told Mr Ogilvie that he was "too deeply pledged to these men to be able to withdraw with honour" (*Citizen Lord* p 261). Because of the restlessness in the ranks of the Society of United Irishmen he set the 23rd May for the date of rebellion. He was captured on the 19th May, and the following day Lord Castlereagh informed William Wickham that Lord Edward's arrest had had "a considerable effect upon the rebels within the metropolis" (*Citizen Lord* p 274). During the skirmish, Lord Edward stabbed the man who captured him and sometime later the man died. Lord Edward was himself near death and it was told he mentioned 'the mercy of God' and the 'freedom of his country'. He died on the 4th June 1798, in Newgate gaol.

Lord Edward was a good soldier. The American prisoners praised his humanity, later the Iroquois honoured him. Different cultures both recognising his innate goodness. Although his mother kept faith with him to the end, most members of his family did not and this was his misfortune. The privileged Fitzgeralds and their relations had the power to support reform of the Irish Parliament in the crucial years of 1793-95 but after 500 years of Norman Legacy, power came before Justice.

In his will, Lord Edward left his estates to his wife. He rejected primogeniture stating that his property was to be shared equally among his three children. He believed what Thomas Paine wrote that Primogeniture was 'unnatural and unjust'. Lord Edward stayed true to his principles since that day in Paris in 1792 when he renounced his title and shed his aristocratic heritage.

"I would have made an English Lord Edward Fitzgerald" Lord Byron.

'In March 1814 at dinner in the house of entertainer and poet business man and poet Samuel Rogers's house the 26-year-old Lord Byron sat listening to Sheridan talking of the great political upheavals of the 1790s: treason was in the air…Britain and Ireland were shaped by the twin forces of repression and resistance. Byron…an astoundingly successful poet, was overcome with feelings of jealousy and regret. For all his glamour and fame, listening to Sheridan made him feel that he had missed the best time to be alive. He lamented that...he had been but an infant, "If I had been a man," he wrote in his diary that night, "I would have made an English Lord Edward Fitzgerald'" (*A Traitor's Kiss* p 161).

Lord Edward Fitzgerald was of royal blood, a handsome aristocrat, a fervent revolutionary, and in the end a patriot. He believed he could bring equality and freedom to the Irish people. Before his death at the age of 35, he had become a legendary figure, after his death he became forever enshrined as a Romantic hero. For a man with such potential in life, potentiality of greatness and goodness, it was a tragedy that he would be cut off in his prime, and it was a tragedy for Ireland.

I decided to write this chapter after reading Jane's play, *The Visit*, thinking that, somehow, she had Lord Edward Fitzgerald in mind. But that was only the beginning. Soon he led me to a coterie of radical revolutionaries whom Jane would have known of, including Thomas Paine and *The Rights of Man*. She reveals her own, then progressive, ideals through the radical stance of Elizabeth Bennet in *Pride and Prejudice*.

CHAPTER 4

HAPPINESS ON HAMPSHIRE DOWNS

My family had a great love of music and song. Two memories, in particular, have stayed with me. One was my father taking me to the Cork Gramophone Circle when I was four years old where I would sit on the floor listening to Opera. The second was a few years later when my mother and father went to see *A Song to Remember*, a film about the life of Chopin and my mother telling us all about it. Sadly, she died soon afterwards. We grew up with church music, Irish music, classical music and the popular music of the day. Going to the Cork Opera House and to the cinema, where we saw the Hollywood musicals, was important in our lives. My dad and us girls were in a choir. At Christmas, we would always have a night when cousins and neighbours joined in a great singsong.

Once we came of age, the weekend dance was never missed. My sister Margaret liked 'Ceili and Old time' and I sometimes went with her and can still recall as having some of the most enjoyable times of my life. Teresa, preferred Jazz at a place called The Boat Club, while I loved the glamourous Arcadia Ballroom where the big bands played. By the time the baby of our family, Bernadette, at the age of 16, joined us she had the choice of all kinds of dancing and came with each of us. She was an Irish traditional dancer herself and after having won every accolade possible, opened her own dancing school.

The assemblies, balls and impromptu house dances in Jane's novels were like the dances of our youth in Cork City, although ours were less formal and less grand. Both served the purpose of making friends, enjoying the dance, meeting a boyfriend or maybe Mr Right. Preparation, anxiety, and even the fear of being ignored, just like Elizabeth was by Darcy (*PP* p 12) was all part of the evening. We had fun and laughter and the occasional disappointment but we, and our friends, with the elation of youth were back the next week. In the days between we discussed the dance just like the Bennet sisters did in *Pride and Prejudice*.

A love story of Music Song and Dance

Jane Austen's novels are exhilarating, with their many instances of music, song, and dance. They mirrored her own passion for, and enjoyment of, all three in her personal life. Her particular interest in music and love of dance are fascinatingly reflected in her letters which transmit the value she placed on authenticity. Added to this is the reminiscences of Caroline and James' amazing insights into the mornings and evenings of Jane's day. Finally, the knowledge from the book, *Jane Austen's Music*, completes a portrait of Jane and her musical soul. She reached out to the wonderful global nature of music, Irish music included.

'Praise and gratitude by Scotch and Irish airs'

'Elizabeth, easy and unaffected, had been listened to with much more pleasure, though not playing half so well; and Mary, at the end of a long concerto, was glad to purchase praise and gratitude by Scotch and Irish airs, at the request of her younger sisters, who with some of the Lucases and two or three officers joined eagerly in dancing at one end of the room' (*PP* p 25). Showing here the zeal of the young people for some light release and action after enduring a dull performance, Jane Austen compensates with Celtic music signifying its accessibility and stylish pleasure for the dancers.

Irish slow airs were hauntingly romantic but Irish dance music was risqué with a dash of wildness and therefore exciting. It had in its makeup the soul of Ireland. It was also very contemporary, formed in some rural village where few grand instruments were available. The people would use whatever musical means available to accompany their dances, even employing the complex rhythms of the fancy steps themselves in their musical art. If 'some of the Lucases and two or three officers' and the good-looking pleasant Mr Bingley responded by 'eagerly dancing at one end of the room' then the Irish airs that Mary played would have their origins in the countryside of Ireland, especially the Gaelic speaking communities. It was theirs alone, embedded in their very psyche, it was and still is a living tradition. This musical achievement survived and developed in the face of successive invasions of Ireland and was even at times endorsed and appreciated by the invaders.

The Irish preserved dance in times of suppression, and brought it with them in times of exile. It is intrinsic to national identity, and the diaspora of Irish people served to widen its audience as this heritage travelled with the exiles to France, Spain, and other parts of Europe. There it was appreciated for its merit without the social and political aspersion it had held for those who had sought to suppress it.

From the early 18th Century Reels and Hornpipes had become part of the dancing scene not only in Ireland but also in Britain. The violin became a new addition among musicians. In Ireland, it was known as a fiddle, and the fiddler and dance master would travel from place to place where steps would be taught to all social classes. Arthur Young (1780) noted that 'dancing is very general among the poor people…It is an absolute system of education'. Jigs, country dances were also taught, the popular group dance the *Rinca Fada* a combination of dancing and marching was danced until the end of the 19th Century.

The Celtic revival, from Dennis Hempson to Jane Austen.

The sense of native identity was adopted by the incoming settlers as they became more sensitive to Irish culture. In the 1790s the current vogue of Romanticism heralded an aesthetic Celtic Revival and the beauty of traditional Irish melodies was recognised. Many were written down, catalogued and thus survived. Attempts were also made to save what remained of the traditional harp music which was dying out after nearly a thousand years.

In Ireland under the Brehon laws, the old Gaelic chieftains bestowed their aristocratic patronage on their bards and harpers, who in turn recorded in poetry and song, their deeds and triumphs. This elaborate system survived for centuries until it was destroyed by a succession of harshly restrictive legislation dating from Tudor times. Henry VIII declared that the music of the harpers incited rebellion and ordered harps destroyed, yet he retained Irish pipers as part of his military. Elizabeth I issued a decree ordering the execution OF Irish harpers.

Its popular renaissance in the 1790's was largely accomplished by Edward Bunting, a nineteen-year-old student of music at Belfast University. Travelling to places in Connacht and further north, he collected music for the harp, and had luckily, for posterity, visited the blind 95-year-old Dennis Hempson in Derry, who played with long fingernails 'in the best old style' on strings of brass. In July 1792, a Harpers Assembly was held in Belfast and organised by a Dr MacDonnell. He commissioned Bunting to transcribe the music played by the visiting nomadic harpers, and was cautioned to interpret it in its purity. Of the ten Harpers present, only Dennis Hempson played in the traditional way, contributing '*An Chuilfhionn' (The Coolin), Elleen-a-roon,* and *Ceandubhdilis*, all slow airs, and *The Dawning of the Day* which can also be played as a march. Bunting did not interpret the tunes in the character of the Gaelic harp method, and much of its authenticity was lost. Yet he created a document which had a much wider appreciation of Irish musical heritage when in 1796 he published the *General Collection of the Ancient Music of Ireland.*

Years later Thomas Moore, the poet and lyricist, renowned for his romantic compositions, successfully published his first set of *Irish Melodies* in 1807 'and of the sixteen beautiful airs included in that book, at least half were taken from Bunting's book' (*The Life And Poems Of Thomas Moore* p 22). This firmly consolidated centre stage Ireland's rich musical tradition and poetic heritage. The 'airs' have come full circle by now; travelling from Dennis Hempson and the harpers at the Belfast Assembly in 1792, to Edward Bunting's *General Collection of the Ancient Music of Ireland*, to Thomas Moore's *Irish Melodies* and finally to Jane Austen's novel, *Emma*, 1816 where Frank Churchill says to Emma "And here are a new set of Irish Melodies" (*E* p 242).

1800 - The Concert Harp - the vogue in fashionable circles

Jane is referring to the much larger concert harp when she includes musical occasions in her letters and novels. In April 1811, she describes an amazing party at Henry and Eliza's home in London to Cassandra "where eighty-three people" were invited and "At half past seven arrived the Musicians in two Hackney coaches, & by 8 the lordly company began to appear…The music was extremely good. It opened, tell Fanny with 'Polke pe Parp pin praise pof Prapela' - & of the other glees I remember, 'In Peace Love tunes', 'Rosabelle', 'The red cross Knight', & 'Poor Insect'. Between the Songs were Lessons on the Harp, or Harp & Piano Forte together - & the Harp Player was Wiepart, whose name seems famous, tho' new to me, - There was one female singer, a short Miss Davis all in blue…whose voice was said to be very fine indeed; & all the Performers gave great satisfaction by doing what they were paid for" (Lt 70).

The concert harp had become a status symbol by the 1800s and Jane uses it to reveal character and circumstance in her novels. In *Sense and Sensibility* 'The party…comprehended a great many people who had real taste for the performance, and a great many more who had none at all; As Elinor was neither musical, nor affecting to be so, she made no scruple of turning away her eyes from the grand pianoforte…and unrestrained even by the presence of a harp' (*SS* p 250). In *Mansfield Park*, sophisticated Londoner Mary Crawford had to wait for the delivery of her harp until the harvest was gathered and a horse and cart was available to fetch it. Edmund Bertram declared it his favourite instrument but Fanny Price, his cousin, had never heard it played, making clear the distinction between his wealthy status and her poor one. Harp music was central to the perceived stylishly elite culture in the late 18th and 19th Centuries.

In *Emma*, the prying Mrs Elton urges Jane Fairfax to become a governess telling her "Your musical knowledge alone would entitle you to name your own terms…and mix in the family…if you knew the harp, you might do all that' (*E* p 301). Jane Austen is making fun of the affected image-conscious Mrs Elton. In *Persuasion* Louisa and Henrietta Musgrove walk from the Great House to Uppercross cottage, so that the harp can be brought in the carriage for the evening. Their actions lay bare their sham, they are just fashion victims. "I am come on to give you notice, that papa and mamma are out of spirits this evening, especially mamma…And we agreed it would be best to have the harp, for it seems to amuse her more than the piano-forte" (*PER* p 50). Jane had a genuine interest in the forms of music for its own sake and not just for the modern aspects she frequently enjoyed to lampoon.

Jane's musical youth and the Winchester organist

Jane's musical education began in her childhood. At school in Reading she learnt singing and dancing. Growing up in a Rectory she was familiar with the hymns and liturgical music of the time. Her parents became aware of her musical ability, and they had George William Chard (1765-1849) an organist at Winchester Cathedral come to Steventon to give her piano lessons. She writes to Cassandra in 1796 "I am glad to hear so good account of Mr. Chard…I practise every day as much as I can - I wish it were more for his sake" (Lt 4 1796).

Her niece Caroline born in 1805 gives us a fascinating glimpse of Jane, recalling how 'Aunt Jane began her day with music…had a natural taste; as she thus kept it up - tho' she had no one to teach; was never induced…to play in company; and none of her family cared much for it…she chose her practising time before breakfast …practised regularly every morning…played very pretty tunes…I liked to stand by her and listen to them…Much that she played was from manuscript, copied out by herself - and so neatly…that it was as easy to read as print-' (*My Aunt Jane Austen* pp 6/7).

Music may not have been part of the recreation in Jane's home but she did enjoy musical sessions at the homes of friends, especially that of Mrs Lefroy a musician herself. Jane is revealing her own thoughts in *Mansfield Park* when Mary Crawford relates to Edmund and Fanny "I shall be most happy to play to you both…at least, as long as you can like to listen…for I dearly love music myself, and where the natural taste is equal, the player must always be best off, for she is gratified in more ways than one" (*MP* p 59).

In her young writing, Jane makes fun of those pretending musical interest. In *Jack and Alice*, Lucy says "I have lived with her for the last 8 years…she provided me with some of the first rate Masters, who taught me all the accomplishments requisite for one of my sex and rank. I learned Dancing, Music, Drawing & various Languages, by which means I became more accomplished than any other Taylor's Daughter in Wales" (*MW* p 20). In *Lesley Castle* (1791) Jane lays bare the persona of Lady Lesley who "plays, sings and Dances, but has no taste for either, and excels in none, tho' she says she is passionately fond of all" (*MW* p 120).

In her novels, Jane still delights in this pretence of musical interest and creates vivid moments for her characters. In *Emma*, there is a refreshing candour in Harriet's observation, 'I hate Italian singing ...There is no understanding a word of it' (*E* p 232). In *Sense and Sensibility* at the home of Sir John Middleton, Marianne sings 'the chief of the songs which Lady Middleton had brought into the family on her marriage, and which perhaps had lain ever since...on the pianoforte...Marianne's performance was highly applauded, Sir John was loud in his admiration...and as loud in his conversation...while every song lasted. Lady Middleton frequently called him to order, wondered how any one's attention could be diverted from music for a moment, and asked Marianne to sing a particular song which Marianne had just finished' (*SS* p 35).

"I rather wonder now at your knowing any" (*PP* p 39)

Music was a key accomplishment, a vital part of a lady's education and exemplified in Jane's novels. Marianne Dashwood, Elizabeth Bennet, Mary Crawford, Emma Woodhouse, Jane Fairfax, and Anne Elliot are not just pretty, they all sing the romantic songs of the day and play the piano, adding to their attractiveness. Humour is often part of the narrative at the expectation and attainment of such merit. In *Pride and Prejudice* when Mr. Darcy declares he does not know more than half a dozen accomplished women, the snobbish Miss Bingley defines this for him "A woman must have a thorough knowledge of music, singing, drawing, dancing, and the modern languages, to deserve the word" to which Mr. Darcy added "extensive reading" and Elizabeth remarks wittily to him "I am no longer surprised at your knowing only six accomplished women. I rather wonder now at your knowing any" (*PP* p 39).

By contrast, in *Emma*, Jane Fairfax is noted as one of the most 'accomplished young woman in England' to the dismay of Emma who regretted 'the inferiority of her own playing and singing...grieve over the idleness of her childhood - and sat down and practised vigorously an hour and a half' (*E* p 231).

Singing - Let the other ladies have time to exhibit (*PP* p 101).

Jane loved to sing. Her nephew James remembers her 'sweet voice, both in singing and in conversation...In the evening she would sometimes sing, to her own accompaniment, some simple old songs, the words and airs of which...still linger in my memory' (*A Memoir of Jane Austen* p 70). She was aware of her own musical limitations and sensitive to the comedy of those who lacked this self-awareness. In *Pride and Prejudice* Elizabeth's 'performance was pleasing, though by no means capital' (*PP* p 25) but her sister Mary sang for too long, eliciting the penetrating remark from their father "That will do extremely well, child. You have delighted us long enough. Let the other young ladies have time to exhibit" (*PP* p 101).

Music can also uplift and encourage. In *Sense and Sensibility*, the broken-hearted Marianne stared miserably at a copy of the opera containing hers and Willoughby's favourite duets, and where he had inscribed her name. She decided 'That would not do - She shook her head' (*SS* p 342) and began to embrace life again. Music is clearly almost a medium, for conveying a lot about characters as Jane shows in *Persuasion* where anticipation and a sense of occasion play their part in the experience, 'Anne's mind was in a most favourable state for the entertainment of the evening...she had feelings for the tender, spirits for the gay, attention for the scientific, and patience for the wearisome; and had never liked a concert more' (*PER* p 186).

Fond of dancing

The Celtic mood and style influenced Romanticism and inspired music which became part of the popular tunes to dances in Jane's time. Irish airs lent themselves to a more easily replicated musical form, ideal for domestic settings like the small gatherings of family and friends such as Jane and the characters in her novels would have enjoyed. In the home music was performed by a few musicians, making it sociable, and personal.

Dancing was a happy part of Jane's life

Dancing was the most popular form of entertainment. It brought single men and women together where they had opportunities to flirt. Jane delights in this device to evolve plots and relationships in her novels and as the letter below reveals it also brought her much personal pleasure in her own life. When she was twenty she opened the ball at Goodnestone writing to Cassandra, "in the Evening danced two Country Dances and the Boulangeries. - I opened the Ball with Edward Bridges; the other couples, were Lewis Cage & Harriot, Frank and Louisa, Fanny & George. Elizabeth played one

Country dance, Lady Bridges the other…Miss Finch played the Boulangeries", and tells Cassandra that she is "extremely anxious to hear…of your Ball…Let me know how many besides their fourteen Selves…Michael will contrive to place about their Coach, and how many of the Gentlemen, Musicians & Waiters, he will have persuaded to come in their Shooting Jackets…and which of the Marys will carry the day with my Brother James" (Lt 5 1796).

She tells Cassandra that the ball at Manydown, home of their friends was "by no means unpleasant. There were 31 people, and only 11 ladies…There were twenty dances, and I danced them all…I could just as well dance for a week together as for half an hour…I am full of joy at much of your information; that you should have been to a ball…and supped with the Prince" (Lt 15 - 1798).

In 1799 she tells Cassandra, "The ball at Kempshott is this evening, and I have got him (Charles) an invitation". She later writes, "There were more dancers than the room could conveniently hold…People were rather apt not to ask me till they could…I danced with Mr. John Wood again, twice with a Mr. South, a lad from Winchester …with G. Lefroy, and J. Harwood, who, I think takes to me rather more than he used to do. One of my gayest actions was sitting down two dances in preference to having Lord Bolton's eldest son for my partner, who danced too ill to be endured" (Lt 17 Jan.1799).

Dancing was the most popular form of social activity and considered something of an art. The Basingstoke assemblies, balls and dances in the neighbourhood houses, were a part of the social life, and a happy part of Jane's own life. Henry Austen said that Jane 'was fond of dancing and excelled in it' (*Memoirs* p 139). And her nephew James wrote 'There must have been more dancing throughout the country in those days than there is now…sprung up more spontaneously…with less fastidiousness as to the quality of music, lights, and floor…Dinner parties more frequently ended with an extempore dance…to the music of a harpsichord in the house, or a fiddle from the village. This was always supposed to be for the entertainment of the young people, but many, who had little pretension to youth, were very ready to join in it. There can be no doubt that Jane herself enjoyed dancing, for she attributes this taste to her favourite heroines; in most of her novels, a ball or a private dance is mentioned, and made of importance' (*Memoirs* p 32).

The musical style of such occasions is commented on. The stately Minuet opened every ball and 'Hornpipes Reels and Cotillons were occasionally danced; but the chief occupation of the evening was the…country dance…The ladies and gentlemen were ranged apart from each other in opposite rows, so that the facilities for flirtation, or interesting intercourse, were not so great' (*Memoirs* pp 33/34).

Dancing in her novels

What Jane experienced in her own life is woven into her novels. Her realistic descriptions of assemblies, balls, house dances could not have been so authentic without herself having being an authority and participator as much as an acute observer during her life.

Jane narrates 'To be fond of dancing was a certain step towards falling in love; and very lively hopes of Mr Bingley's heart were entertained' (*PP* p 9). Jane even has Mr Tilney, in *Northanger Abbey* use dance as an analogy, declaring, "I consider a country-dance as an emblem of marriage. Fidelity and complaisance are the principal duties of both" (*NA* p 76).

Fanny's first ball in *Mansfield Park*, was, 'without, the preparation or splendour of many a young lady's first ball, being the thought only of the afternoon, built on the late acquisition of a violin player …and the possibility of raising five couple' (*MP* p 117). In *Persuasion* 'The girls were wild for dancing; and the evenings ended…in an unpremeditated little ball. There was a family of cousins…they would…dance anywhere; and Anne…played country dances to them by the hour together' (*PER* p 47).

Moreover, like an irresistible rhythm itself, one thing leads to another, so while visiting the Coles in *Emma*, 'Miss Bates…put an end to all further singing…for Miss Woodhouse and Miss Fairfax were the only young-lady-performers; but soon the proposal of dancing…Mrs. Weston, capital in her country dances, was seated, and beginning an irresistible waltz; and Frank Churchill, coming up with most becoming gallantry to Emma, had secured her hand…led off the dance with genuine spirit and enjoyment. Not more than five couple could be mustered; but the rarity and the suddenness of it made it very delightful' (*E* 229/230).

It is the ball, around which the social life, passions, and reputations reverberate. In *Pride and Prejudice*, 'If there had not been a Netherfield ball to prepare for and talk of, the younger Miss Bennets would have been in a pitiable state...Even Elizabeth might have found some trial of her patience...and nothing less than a dance on Tuesday, could have made such a Friday, Saturday, Sunday and Monday, endurable to Kitty and Lydia' (*PP* p 88).

Such musical occasions enable Jane to reveal what the characters are like. In *Pride and Prejudice*, the behaviour on the dance floor, reveal the polished wit and touchy assertions of Elizabeth Bennet and Darcy. Charlotte cautions Elizabeth 'not to be a simpleton and allow her fancy for Wickham make her appear unpleasant in the eyes of a man of ten times his consequence' while 'Elizabeth made no answer...took her place in the set, amazed...in being allowed to stand opposite to Mr. Darcy...They stood for some time without speaking...and she began to imagine that their silence was to last ...and...was resolved not to break it' (*PP* 90/91).

"No - I cannot talk of books in a ball-room!"

Jane's life was a dance, Jane makes this a metaphor for almost all that is joyful and fun in life. It is hard not to imagine her enthusiasm for dancing, as she has Elizabeth delightfully say to Darcy "No - I cannot talk of books in a ball-room; my head is always full of something else" (*PP* p 93). While after their musical encounter, Darcy is left with a, 'tolerable powerful feeling towards her' (*PP* p 94). Jane's unfinished novel *The Watsons* comments on the 'bliss and brilliancy' of a ball and has Elizabeth Watson say to her sister Emma "I am sure I should never have forgiven the person who kept me from a Ball at 19" (*MW* p 320). In *Mansfield Park* the sober Fanny can find delight in the dance, 'The ball...an evening of pleasure before her! and she began to dress for it with much of the happy flutter which belongs to a ball' (*MP* p 270), and once 'in the ball-room, the violins were playing, and her mind was in a flutter that forbade its fixing on anything serious' (*MP* p 275).

Music, and it's playing, can give expression to deep emotions. Anne Elliot in *Persuasion*, as an older unmarried woman, is subject to social condescension in addition to her own anguish at having lost her love, both revealed when the evening ends with dancing. 'Anne offered her services...and though her eyes would sometimes fill with tears as she sat at the instrument, she was extremely glad to be employed, and desired nothing in return but to be unobserved ...These were some of the thoughts which occupied Anne, while her fingers were mechanically at work...Once she felt that he was looking at herself - observing her altered features, perhaps, trying to trace in them the ruins of the face which had once charmed him; and once she knew that he must have spoken of her...she heard the answer..."Oh! No, never; she has quite given up dancing. She had rather play'" *(PER pp 71/72)*.

Regent Street - Christmas Sales and Jane Austen's Music

One day I went with a friend of mine, Charlie, to the Christmas sales and discovered the book, *Jane Austen's Music* in a shop called 'Past Times' in Regent Street. This was a happy day for me and soon this chapter became my favourite one. For weeks, I sifted through the book's pages again and again. It tells of Jane's music collection at Chawton which include over 300 works, much of it copied out by hand. It has keyboard sonatas, arias and cantatas, solos for keyboard from orchestral music and from Italian operas. It includes music from over 70 composers, both present and past and representing nearly every European country. There is music by Arne, Arnold, Boyce, Hook and Jackson, and Linley; Dibdin and Shield, who apparently wrote for the Anglican liturgy, and for the stage. Music from Purcell, Handel, Haydn, Steibelt, and Mozart are in her collection. Jane's glamorous cousin Eliza de Feuillide, another lover of music may have given her compositions by Pleyel, French songs and a copy of the Marseillaise.

Music in the late 18th and early 19th centuries represented the current culture of Romantic era which is emotional and linked to the cult of the sublime. Nature is seen as awe inspiring and beyond control like the sweeping grandeur of Beethoven against the music of a more rigid past seen in the orderly melody of Handel, both "Majestic" but in different ways. Jane's musical collection reflects these trends.

One of the piano pieces in her collection, copied out by Jane herself in the 1790s, is *My Lodging is on the Cold Ground*. It is also duet 'used by Richard Sheridan in *The Rivals*' (p 15). Its beautiful melody is the same one which, 10 years later, Thomas Moore used for his sentimental song, 'Believe me, if all those endearing young charms' in his *Irish Melodies* (1807). There is a song called *Susan* (p 61) which could be traced to Sheridan's 1794 The Glorious 1st of June Benefit, held at Drury Lane in aid of the widows and orphans of the men who died in Lord Howe's victory out in the Atlantic. In the production, the sailor's name is William and the girl's name is Susan. Jane herself used these names in *Mansfield Park*, where William a midshipman is Fanny's brother and Susan her sister.

Along with comic songs and excerpts from musicals of the day; there are daring waltzes and Scottish songs. There is the Mary Queen of Scots song *Beyond Dull Care* (p 5) a link with Jane's *History of England*. Jane must have shared the nursery song *Goosey Goosey Gander* (p 62) with her many nieces and nephews. Unsurprisingly given Jane's affection for her sailor brothers, there are many sea shanties and sailor songs in her manuscripts.

This nautical tradition of song was influenced by Irish Culture. Many of the sailors were Irish with a love of singing their native songs whose catchy tunes became very popular. Melodies were used in the working life of the ship. The engine of the ship was the men, who performed certain tasks like pulling anchor to a rhythmic beat. The sentimental ballads and shanties reflected their emotions - homesickness, misery of leaving womenfolk, romance of faraway shores, perils of the sea, and warfare created their own signature music. Patriotic songs were sung, giving support for the growing navy. Dances like the Hornpipe were becoming popular and they reflect directly back to their mostly Irish roots. *The Good Ship Kangaroo* and *The Irish Rover* are sea shanties of this time.

Among her music was *The African Song* telling the story of the Scottish explorer Mungo Park who was the first European to trace the course of the Niger river. He lost his way and was given a bed for the night by a kind-hearted woman who with her female relatives sang a song about his plight to Mandinka music. On his return to England he had a version published. There is also the *Hindoo Girl's Song* from Hindustan. These two songs show the universal perspective of Jane.

Her collection surprises in its depth of soul; having two of the most treasured items in the ancient Catholic hymnals. One is the hymn of the Sicilian Mariners, *O Sanctissima, O piissima dulcis Virgo* (p 44) the other is the Benediction antiphon, *O Salutaris Hostia* (p 43), attributed to Samuel Webbe (1740-1816). It shows her appreciation of aspects of the Roman Catholic liturgy.

Much Irish music in Jane's collection

With such a musical soul, it was natural that Jane would gravitate to Irish music. Amongst her Manuscripts are many Irish tunes including the beautiful slow air *The Coolin* (p 56). Music publishing flourished in Dublin from the 1750s onwards. Benjamin Rhames printed sheet music from 1756 to 1775. Its songs were sung by an Irish singer "Mr Johnstone". Another Irish element was the working partnership from the early 1790's between the English composer William Shield and the Irish impresario J. O'Keefe, whose songs were in circulation around 1795. Longman & Broderip printed fashionable collections of dance music, reels, Scots and Irish' (p 49). The Hime family from 1790 onwards produced songs from 'stage works, instrumental arrangements of country dances and Irish Airs' (p 50). Perhaps, while her brothers' sailing duties took them to Ireland they acquired music for their sister. Several pieces in her third manuscript book are from Irish publications.

Irish music promoted the sentiment and consciousness of being Irish, which whilst politically pertinent and particularly volatile in the 1790's also offered a deliciously Romantic and heroic stereotype. A popular song of this time *The Irishman* (pp 16,44,59) reinforces this typecast in a mock ballad where the various nationalities can only provide lovers who are to be seen as "wanting" in comparison to the irresistible charms of an Irishman.

"The London Folks themselves beguile
And think they please in a capital stile
Yet let them ask as they cross the street
Of any young virgin they happen to meet
And I know she'll say, from behind her fan
That there's none can love like an Irishman, like an Irishman.
     (The British Minstrel and National Melodist, pp 265-266, Sherwood, Gilbert and Piper,1827.)

It is tempting to speculate whether this piece of music was a gift from Jane's own particular Irishman, Tom Lefroy. Fashion and personal taste coincide, and an unforgettable association with Ireland is likely to have been forged for Jane.

We can only imagine what music Jane had in mind as she wrote her novels. We now know that she had 300 works to choose from. The life of the instrument, song and dance is the life of Jane Austen's novels. When music is played or a song is sung or the dancers are enjoying themselves any item from Jane's collection of musical manuscripts could be part of the repertoire.

There are three direct references to Irish music in her novels. In *Pride and Prejudice*" 'Mary…was glad to purchase praise and gratitude by Scotch and Irish airs' (*PP* p 25). In *Northanger Abbey* John Thorpe asks Catherine if she heard of the old song "Going to one wedding brings on another?" (*NA* p 123). Here Jane had in mind the Irish ditty called *Old Maid in the Garret*. In *Emma*, Frank Churchill points to a "new set of Irish Melodies" (*E* p 242). They are all connected with Ireland, showing Jane's search for the genuine.

Jane delighted in, and enjoyed, music which exemplified the spirit of the age. Her music collection is a legacy to us. For over thirty years of her life she collected her 'eight bound volumes' part of it in manuscript, a labour of love for music, amongst which were many Irish compositions devotedly copied out by Jane Austen herself.

CHAPTER 5

IN SEARCH OF PRIDE AND PREJUDICE

The mystery of Richard Sheridan's play (*The Rivals*) and Jane Austen's novel (*Pride and Prejudice*) took me some years to solve and many an evening I studied both together. The moment of illumination came to me when I saw a clear link between the epilogue in his play and the opening sentence in her novel.

In *The Rivals* Sheridan muses on the power of women in his epilogue

'One moral's plain - cried I - without more fuss;
Man's social happiness all rest on us -
Through all the drama - whether damned or not -
Love gilds the scene, and women guide the plot.
From every rank obedience is our due -
D'ye doubt? - the world's great stage shall prove it true'…
The surly squire at noon resolves to rule,
And half the day - 'Zounds! Madam is a fool!'
Convinced at night - the vanquished victor says,
'Ah! Kate you women have such coaxing ways!'…

Jane's opening sentence in *Pride and Prejudice* begins with similar sagacity, 'It is a truth universally acknowledged that a single man in possession of a good fortune, must be in want of a wife. However little known the feelings or views of such a man may be on his first entering a neighbourhood, this truth is so well fixed in the minds of the surrounding families, that he is considered as the rightful property of someone or other of their daughters' (*PP* p 3).

Jane's lure of the rich man needing a wife contrasts with Sheridan's epilogue that men whatever their station in life, depend on woman for their happiness. In Jane's introduction riches are stressed whereas in Sheridan's epilogue feminine wiles are stressed, but both make humorous comment on the necessity of marriage and the genuine roles of women.

Both *The Rivals* and *Pride and Prejudice* are the early works of their authors. Sheridan, newlywed, hurriedly wrote his play at the age of twenty-four. William Hazlitt, a theatre critic of the time wrote that *The Rivals* works far better on stage than in study. Jane Austen had the advantage of seeing it performed when a very young girl. *The Rivals* which is high comedy takes place in the course of one day in the city of Bath, while *Pride and Prejudice* spans a year in the counties of Hertfordshire, Kent and Derbyshire.

In his play, Sheridan used influences from a variety of sources. He created the hilarious Mrs Malaprop (a name which gave way to "malapropism", a word now in the English dictionary) using elements from his mother's play A Journey to Bath as well as Dogberry from Shakespeare's Much Ado About Nothing, and Fielding's Mrs Slipslop. The country Squire Bob Acres has facets of Tony Lumpkin from Oliver Goldsmith's *She Stoops to Conquer*.

In *The Rivals* Captain Jack Absolute loves the rich and beautiful Lydia Languish but senses that he has little chance of winning her because her head is full of silly notions from all the romantic fiction she has read. She meets Ensign Beverley, "likes him better as a half-pay ensign" (I, i) and imagines herself eloping with him, but is unaware that he is really Captain Jack Absolute, in a disguise to win her love. Eventually he is caught out.

Hidden in the narrative of *Pride and Prejudice* is Sheridan's *The Rivals*

Jane Austen based her *Pride and Prejudice* on the structure of *The Rivals* using its plotline for her own matrix of characters. From Lydia

Languish she creates two sisters, Lydia Bennet who is wayward and ignorant and Elizabeth Bennet who is lively and intelligent. Jane has the glamourous Mr Darcy in place of Captain Jack Absolute and brings 'Ensign Beverley' to life in the creation of the anti-hero George Wickham.

In the same way that Sheridan selects and contrasts his couples, Jane Austen closely connects with him as she conceives the various partnerships of her characters. She speculates possible outcomes for Sheridan's Lydia Languish whose initial wish was to marry her poor 'Ensign Beverley'. Jane has the answer in Lydia Bennet who meets her fate when she eventually marries the smarmy but ruthless Wickham who has "the promise of an ensigncy in General--'s regiment, now quartered in the North" (p 312).

The moment that Jane makes Sheridan's "Ensign Beverley" come alive as Wickham

The Bennet sisters visit the village of Meryton and meet Denny, one of the officers who introduce Wickham, a new recruit to Kitty and Lydia who remark that he 'only wanted regimentals to make him completely charming' (p 72). Just at that moment Mr Darcy and Mr Bingley enter the village on horseback and ride slowly towards them. Briefly, Mr Darcy and Wickham exchange looks and Elizabeth witnessed the astonishment and recognition in their faces. 'Both changed colour, one looked white, the other red. Mr Wickham…touched his hat - a salutation which Mr Darcy just deigned to return', Elizabeth, watching, wondered 'at the meaning of it?' (p 73). This is the moment that Jane makes Sheridan's "Ensign Beverley" come alive in the creation of Wickham, but throughout her novel she never allows Darcy and Wickham to communicate directly and this culminates in a revealing sentence towards its closing, 'Though Darcy could never receive him at Pemberley…Lydia was occasionally a visitor there, when her husband was gone to enjoy himself in London or Bath' but both of them stayed so long with the Bingleys that 'his good humour was overcome' (p 387).

The couples of the sub-plot begin the action in play and novel

In both *The Rivals* and *Pride and Prejudice* the couples of the sub-plot begin the action. In *The Rivals* Julia and Faulkland are an established couple but he is suffering from doubts as to her sincerity. He has the reality of Julia but is silly enough to desire 'appearances' and he wallows in fashionable romantic uncertainties. In *Pride and Prejudice* Jane Bennet a 'sweet girl' and Mr Bingley love each other, but are parted by the scheming of others. Bingley who is easily influenced, fails to act on his own feelings preferring the opinions of others. Both couples, mainly through their lack of initiative remain estranged until the final scene and chapter, when mistakes are resolved and they can marry. Julia's guardian Sir Anthony Absolute, and Jane's father Mr Bennet make points at the end of play and novel. Sir Anthony says to Julia that Faulkland's faults "proceed from…the delicacy and warmth of his affection for you…marry him directly Julia; you'll find he'll mend surprisingly!" (V, iii). Mr Bennet congratulates Jane and Bingley telling her that she will be a very happy woman, and he has no doubt of their "doing very well together…You are each of you so complying, that nothing will ever be resolved on!" (p 348).

Kitty Bennet in *Pride and Prejudice* is modelled on Lucy the maid in *The Rivals*. Sheridan introduces Lydia Languish and her maid Lucy in the respective roles of mistress and servant. Lucy says 'commend me to a mask of silliness and a pair of sharp eyes…to what account have I turned my simplicity lately. For abetting Miss Lydia Languish in a design of running away with an ensign!' (I, ii).

In *Pride and Prejudice* Jane Austen places Lydia Bennet and her sister Kitty in a position similar to that of Lydia Languish and Lucy. They are referred to by their father as, "two of the silliest girls in the country" (p 29) who spend most of their time in Meryton, 'dallying with the officers resplendent in the regimentals of an ensign' (p 29). Throughout the novel Lydia and Kitty are close, and their 'misery was extreme' (p 229) when the regiment was ordered to the seaside town of Brighton (p 229). Then Lydia leaves for Brighton (p 235) and writes to Kitty of her romance and expected elopement with Ensign Wickham (p 290). This echoes Lucy's knowledge of the hoped-for elopement of her mistress Lydia Languish and 'Ensign Beverley' in *The Rivals*. Just like Lucy the maid, Kitty Bennet is also a "silly" accomplice.

Books, a shower of rain and a dance are features in play and novel

One of the first connections I made between *The Rivals* and *Pride and Prejudice* is the incident concerning books. In *The Rivals* as Lydia Languish is enjoying a romantic novel she hears Mrs Malaprop and Sir Anthony Absolute, her prospective Father-in-law, approaching and tells Lucy to hide several books, "fling Peregrine Pickle under the toilet - throw Roderick Random into the closet…and leave Fordyce's Sermons open on the table" (I, ii). There is a comparable incident in *Pride and Prejudice* as Mr Bennet invites Mr Collins 'to read aloud to the ladies' handing him a book from a circulating library. Mr Collins 'protested that he never read novels' which brought an astonished reaction from Kitty and Lydia. He then chooses Fordyce's Sermons and after reading 'three pages' Lydia interrupted him but 'was bid by her two eldest sisters to hold her tongue; but Mr Collins…laid aside his book saying "I have often observed how little young ladies are interested by books of a serious stamp" (pp 68/69). Once again it is only Kitty and Lydia react in a situation reminiscent of 'Fordyce's Sermons' in Sheridan's play.

Rain is another connection in play and novel. Faulkland is teased by Absolute that he should, 'love like a man' when he is in a state of anxiety, fearing for Julia's 'spirits and health', "If it rains, some shower may even then have chilled her delicate frame!" (11,i). Jane, in her novel emulates this incident. The Bingley sisters invite Jane Bennet to dine with them at their Netherfield home and Mrs Bennet insist on her riding there. But Jane is exposed to a heavy shower of rain and becomes ill with a fever. Consequently, she is confined to bed at Netherfield for several days and Bingley's 'anxiety for Jane was evident' (p 35).

Further correlation is provided by a dance. Faulkland is upset that Julia was 'country-dancing' in his absence and says to Absolute "Country dances! Jigs and reels!…A minuet I could have forgiven…but…to run the gauntlet through a string of amorous palming puppies!…Oh, Jack, there never can be but one man in the world whom a truly modest and delicate woman ought to pair with in a country-dance; and even then, the rest of the couples should be her great- uncles and aunts!" (11, i). In contrast Bingley is shown to love dancing, partnering Jane at their first meeting at the Meryton

Assembly, and at the Netherfield Ball he danced all the evening with her. At the Lucas's party, he joined Lydia and Kitty with 'some of the Lucases' in dancing (p 25) and this time Jane Bennet did not take part. Was she too lady-like for such dancing? as Faulkland believed Julia should have been in *The Rivals*.

Heroes and heroines need to find the right partners

Sheridan's rich heroine Lydia Languish and Jane's rich hero Mr Darcy in *Pride and Prejudice* both need to find the right partner but there are dilemmas to be solved along the way concerning the nature of romantic love, the realities of finance, the problems of mistaken identity and above all the ability to discern appearances.

Both Sheridan and Jane Austen allow their heroines the freedom to accept or reject proposals of marriage, and neither Captain Absolute nor Mr Darcy are allowed to take for granted, the acceptance of their proposals. Lydia Languish is justifiably annoyed when she realises Absolute is not her "beloved Beverley", while Elizabeth Bennet finds Mr Darcy's opinion on the inferiority of her family and his 'treatment' of Wickham 'insufferable' and tells him that he was "the last man in the world whom I could ever be prevailed on to marry" (p 193). It is this initial rejection and setback to their assumptions that forces declarations and proof of true love from Captain Absolute and Mr Darcy. Absolute is reduced to confessing to Lydia that, "I promise you - If I have lost your heart, I resign the rest" (1V ii) and later has to risk his life in agreeing to fight a duel because of her. Likewise, Mr Darcy has to confront his innermost feelings and reveal them to Elizabeth in what might be a compromise of his social standing. He sacrifices himself in her interest when he confronts Wickham who has treacherously mortified his family. Then he attests his love for her. So, both heroes must prove their honour to be worthy of the women they will marry.

The heroines while learning about the nature of love and faced with choices concerning their ideal man versus the real one, also discover truths about themselves. Lydia Languish is rich but lacks wisdom. Elizabeth Bennet is wise but lacks money. They both learn from their mistakes to discriminate between appearance and reality which demands self-knowledge too. Lydia was deluded and chose 'Ensign Beverley' who had the desirable 'appearance', realising later that she really loved Captain Absolute who was the reality. Elizabeth allowed herself to be deceived by her first impressions and almost mistakes Mr Darcy, the ideal, for the worst of men.

Captain Absolute's feelings for Lydia Languish were genuine when he disguised himself as 'Ensign Beverley' to win her. In the novel after Elizabeth and Mr Darcy had come together, Elizabeth says to him "in spite of the pains you took to disguise yourself, your feelings were always noble and just" (p 381).

The comical episodes of tiresome suitors - Bob Acres and Mr Collins

A comparison can also be traced between the roles of Squire Bob Acres, who wants to marry Lydia Languish, and Mr Collins who proposes to Elizabeth Bennet. Bob Acres under the control of his mother, "ancient madam" comes to Bath, establishes himself as a man of style, adopting flowery language and attempting to dance. However, Lydia "is so obstinate against him" that he eventually gets his "discharge" (I ii). The awful suitor in *Pride and Prejudice* is Mr Collins who also has an 'ancient madam' in his life, his patroness, Lady Catherine de Bourgh. He makes his appearance at the Netherfield Ball where his mindless dancing with Elizabeth gave her 'shame and misery' (p 90).

Sheridan ridicules the silliness of Mrs Malaprop worrying over "dear Sir Lucius" being drawn "into the scrape" (v, i). Jane Austen in a similar way, to highlight the ridiculous, has Mrs Bennet despair that Mr Bennet "will fight Wickham…be killed, and what is to become of us all?" (p 287).

The two Lydia's thwarted dreams of elopement

Both play and novel mention an elopement to Scotland. When Sheridan's heroine Lydia Languish finds out that her "Ensign Beverley" is Captain Absolute in disguise, her delusions of romance, and her hopes for a sentimental elopement to Scotland are over, "with…such paragraphs in the newspaper!". For a time she despairs believing she will be a "mere Smithfield bargain" in an arranged marriage to Absolute (v, i).

Sixteen-year-old Lydia Bennet believed she was eloping to Scotland when she ran away with Wickham. Jane Austen was fulfilling the thwarted dreams projected by the sixteen-year-old Lydia

Languish. Lydia Bennet ends up in London and her immature self-knowledge cannot appreciate the irony that, her marriage at St Clements (p 318), close to Smithfield, has in effect been "arranged" through the patronage and patience of Mr Darcy, and what she describes as the "good joke" of signing herself Lydia Wickham is sadly on herself (p 291). Mrs Bennet says that the "wedding was in the Times and the Courier…though it was not put in as it ought to be. It was only said, 'Lately, George Wickham, Esq. To Miss Lydia Bennet', without there being a syllable said of her father, or the place where she lived, or anything" (p 336).

The eyes so innocently wild - the beautiful expression of her dark eyes

There are coincidences of imagery in the two texts as well. In *The Rivals* Sir Anthony raves about Lydia's eyes to his son Jack, "such eyes…so innocently wild! So bashfully irresolute! Not a glance but speaks and kindles some thought of love!" (III, i), and "her eyes shall be the Promethean torch to you" (III, ii). In *Pride and Prejudice* Darcy observed that Elizabeth Bennet 'had hardly a good feature in her face, then he began to find it was rendered uncommonly intelligent by the beautiful expression of her dark eyes' (p 23). He says to Miss Bingley "I have been meditating on the very great pleasure which a pair of fine eyes in the face of a pretty woman can bestow" (p 27).

Absolute

Captain Absolute is the hero of *The Rivals* and Jane Austen uses the words 'absolute' and 'absolutely' many times in her novel and relates them to Mr Darcy. At the Netherfield Ball, Denny stated 'the absolute fact of 'Wickham's absence was "to avoid" Darcy (p 89). When Elizabeth and Darcy meet at Pemberley 'Their eyes instantly met…He absolutely started' (p 251). When Elizabeth tells Darcy about Lydia and Wickham's elopement he says "I am grieved…But is it certain, absolutely certain?" (p 277).

Duelling and deeds of integrity

There is duelling in the play and deeds of integrity in the novel. In the climax of *The Rivals* Captain Absolute's fate is in the balance. He is prepared to risk his life for Lydia by fighting a duel not only on his own behalf, but also of his alias 'Ensign Beverley'. Near the close of the play Absolute's heroism and worthiness are sanctioned by Lydia who is now freed from her false ideas of love and offers "this gentleman my hand, and solicit the return of his affections" (v, iii). Mr Darcy, unlike Absolute, is not called upon to fight duels, but to prove his integrity, he sets about finding Wickham and Lydia and insist they marry. All this is accomplished without involving any of the Bennet family. Darcy's compassion, generosity and humility leads him back to Elizabeth. In a spirit of comedy and a love of irony shared with Sheridan, Jane Austen has Elizabeth writing to her aunt "I am the happiest creature in the world...I am happier even than Jane; she only smiles, I laugh" (pp 382/383).

Jane's greatest game of charades

Jane Austen and her family were very fond of playing charades, and in *Pride and Prejudice* that is just what Jane is doing, hiding *The Rivals* in its narrative. At the age of twenty, and beginning her mature work, she was able to bring one of her great skills into her brilliant writing. Is it any wonder that one of the most enjoyable novels ever written had Sheridan advise 'a Miss Shirreff to buy it immediately, for it was one of the cleverest things he had read' (*Jane Austen* M. Laski p 86)? Did he ever have any inkling that it was from his play that Jane Austen conceived her wonderful, world loved, *Pride and Prejudice*?

CHAPTER 6

MR DARCY TO THE 4TH EARL FITZWILLIAM

Jane used her superb skill with charades to point us to the 4th Earl Fitzwilliam as the model for her creation of the romantic hero Mr Darcy in *Pride and Prejudice.* The use of the word 'savage' always perplexed me. When Sir William Lucas says to Darcy that he considers dancing "one of the first refinements of polished societies" Darcy replies, "Certainly, Sir; - and it has the advantage also of being in vogue amongst the less polished societies of the world. Every savage can dance" (*PP* p 25). Why did Jane draw our attention to the word 'savage', it seemed out of place? Then, one day on a research visit to the British Library I picked up a book called The Collins Peerage and got my answer. Glancing at the particulars of Earl Fitzwilliam's family tree, I saw that that the Family crest included two club wielding "savages". I was surprised and shocked as I realized that this was one of Jane's charades. She was acknowledging the 4th Earl. Now Mr Darcy's words did not seem so strange at all.

In 1786 when she was only eleven years old, Jane Austen wrote an entry in her father's Parish Register 'The banns of marriage between Henry Frederic Howard Fitzwilliam of London and Jane Austen of Steventon'. Ten years later, at the age of twenty she began writing *Pride and Prejudice,* and modelled its romantic hero, Mr Darcy (Fitzwilliam Darcy) on another member of the Fitzwilliam family. He was the 4th Earl Fitzwilliam (1748-1833) of the Peerage of Ireland and 2nd Earl Fitzwilliam of the Peerage of Great Britain. He was one of the richest landowners in England; and owned its largest and grandest stately home, Wentworth Woodhouse in Yorkshire. The Earl was well known and esteemed for his personal qualities too, not least a profound social conscience. In later life, it was said that king George III spoke of him 'with great warmth and esteem'.

The 4th Earl became the Lord Lieutenant of Ireland in 1795

Jane may have felt a special sympathy for the 4th Earl Fitzwilliam when he was brought to great public prominence in 1795 because of his recall in disgrace from his short Lieutenancy in Ireland by Prime Minister William Pitt. The Earl was made Lord Lieutenant in late 1794, to promote a sense of unity in the country. He was a frequent visitor to Ireland. He was convinced of his friend Edmund Burke's passionate conviction that Catholic emancipation, and the end of political control by the Protestant ascendancy, could bring about peace and avert the threat of a French invasion. During his Lord Lieutenancy, the Earl deplored the political injustices carried out against the Catholics. He was compassionate to their needs and attempted to pave the way for their emancipation but failed in his mission. He lived to see the Catholics gain emancipation in 1829.

A day of hope for Ireland when the 4th Earl arrived in Dublin

The Earl arrived in Dublin on January 4th 1795, and was welcomed by eager crowds full of hope that at last Ireland was to have reform. He believed he would succeed in Ireland by putting Whig principles to work and supporting reform of the Catholic Relief Bill (launched in February 1795) to rectify injustice. He faced the challenge of working through the vested interests of the Protestant ascendancy and their Westminster chiefs, as well as his wife's Irish political family, the Ponsonbys, who had estates in Counties Cork and Kilkenny, with the equivalent parliamentary influence.

Aware that the Catholics on the country estates were growing restless and arming themselves against the Protestants, he planned to have them admitted to the yeomanry but the Protestants objected to this move. Earl Fitzwilliam then tried to prepare the Irish Parliament for Catholic emancipation but the Irish Lords most notably Fitzgibbon and Beresford challenged him. He made an error of judgement when he dismissed them and other officials, and their protest to King George III resulted in his recall to London on February 19th 1795.

A day of despair for Ireland as the Earl's carriage was drawn through the streets of Dublin

He left Dublin on March 25th 1795. In his short time as Lord Lieutenant of Ireland he had won the affection of the people, both Catholics and Protestants and they were saddened at his leaving 'The day of his departure was one of general gloom; the shops were shut...and the greater part of the citizens put on mourning, while some of the most respectable among them drew his coach down to the water-side' (*Life of Pitt* Stanhope p 365).The Earl returned to England, disgraced, disillusioned and humiliated. The reformers in Ireland bitterly resented his recall, and were frustrated and repressed by the policies of his replacement, the rigid Lord Camden. Many resorted to more prompt action which culminated in the Rebellion of 1798.

Edmund Burke's letter to a 'Noble Lord' followed the Earl's recall

In the wake of Earl Fitzwilliam's recall from Ireland, the Irish statesman and British politician, Edmund Burke, who was the Earl's friend since their schooldays at Eton, wrote a public letter to him in 1796 addressing him as his 'Noble friend' Fitzwilliam (Letter to a Noble Lord 1796). Jane Austen would have been familiar with this letter and the Parliamentary debates and arguments that followed the Earl's recall. At Westminster, he was going through all the acrimonious backlash from his time in Ireland. It continued through 1795 and 1796. Jane may have felt sympathy for this great Whig magnate because of the manner in which he was treated. She and her family read the newspapers including The Hampshire Chronicle which Mr Holder of Ashe Park passed to Mr. Austen allowing Jane to follow events in Parliament. About this time the twenty-year-old Jane begins to write *Pride and Prejudice* and ascribes the qualities of the 4th Earl Fitzwilliam to her Mr Darcy.

Earl Fitzwilliam and the making of his literary counterpart Mr Darcy

An affinity, not only of position but also of attitude, can be identified between Earl Fitzwilliam and his literary counterpart Mr Darcy. The Romanticism and level-headedness which underpin the construction of Mr Darcy as a heroic character, reflect Earl Fitzwilliam's political and personal loyalty to the Whig party. These principles, which Earl Fitzwilliam demonstrated in practice to the detriment of his own political career, set him apart, then and now, as an example of rare integrity and idealism worthy of such literary translation for Jane's romantic hero in *Pride and Prejudice*.

The "abominable" pride of Mr Darcy - and the Earl's Achilles heel, his pride

The 4th Earl Fitzwilliam's proud nature was his greatest fault. Jane Austen, throughout *Pride and Prejudice*, continually exposes Mr Darcy's 'abominable pride' (p 193).

She is genuinely keeping to the Earl's character. The 4th Earl went through a time of humiliation on his return to England. Jane has Mr Darcy go through some humiliation throughout the novel. This is Jane Austen, she has to be authentic.

At the Assembly, Mr Darcy 'soon drew the attention of the room by his fine, tall person, handsome features, noble mien; and the report which was in general circulation within five minutes after his entrance, of his having ten thousand a year' (p 10).

He was greatly admired until 'he was discovered to be proud' and 'above his company' then everybody began to dislike him and 'hoped that he would never come there again' (p 11). Mrs Bennet was 'most violent' against him because he was heard to say that Elizabeth her daughter, was not 'handsome enough to tempt' him to dance. Mr Darcy was summed up as being 'haughty reserved, and fastidious, and his manners, though well bred, were not inviting' (p 16). George Wickham tells Elizabeth that "almost all" Mr Darcy's actions "may be traced to pride" and it has "led him to be liberal and generous, to give his money freely, to display hospitality, to assist his tenants, and relieve the poor" (p 81). Mrs Gardiner 'recollected...Mr Fitzwilliam Darcy...spoken of as a very proud, ill-natured boy' (p 143). Elizabeth says to Wickham "Mr Darcy improved on acquaintance...from knowing him better, his disposition was better understood" (p 234). At Pemberley Mr Darcy invites Mr Gardiner 'to fish there as often as he chose...offering...to supply him with fishing tackle, and pointing out those parts of the stream where there was usually most sport' (p 255). Mrs Gardiner remarks to Elizabeth "some people may call him proud, I have seen nothing of it" (p 257). Wickham persuades Lydia Bennet to run away to London with him but Mr Darcy saves her 'in a cause of compassion and honour' (p 326). Mr. Darcy 'was the person to whom the whole family were indebted' (p 334) yet he insisted to Mr Gardiner that none of what he did was to be told to Mr Bennet.

Eventually Mr Darcy talks of his 'mistaken pride' to Elizabeth (p 322) and admits that he 'was given good principles but left to follow them in pride and conceit' (p 369). When Elizabeth tells her father of her love for Mr Darcy who has "no improper pride" (p 376), he emerges from being disliked, slandered, and misjudged, to a man of honour, generosity and principle just like the 4th Earl Fitzwilliam was.

Earl Fitzwilliam was a proud man and aware of his status and position. He saw his recall from Ireland as 'a subject of great pain and mortification'. His Lord Lieutenancy was a pivotal moment of hope for the destitute Irish, but Pitt was afraid that the Earl's actions of 'intelligent and measured concession' might compromise the power of his Parliament. So 'the last opportunity to avoid a catastrophic sequence' (*Ireland and the Age of Revolution and Imperialism* 1750-1801 p 458) was lost and the rebellion of 1798 followed.

Mr Collins and Mr Bennet - their praise of Mr Darcy

Mr Collins writes to Mr. Bennet that Mr Darcy "may be reasonably looked up to, as one of the most illustrious personages in this land" (p 362), and Mr. Bennet says "This young gentleman is blessed, in a peculiar way, with everything the heart of mortal man can most desire, - splendid property, noble kindred, and extensive patronage" (p 362). These distinctions can also be attributed to the 4th Earl.

Darcy was the "most generous-hearted boy in the world" - Just like the young Earl was

During their stay in Derbyshire Elizabeth and the Gardiners visit Pemberley the home of Mr Darcy. Mrs Reynolds, the housekeeper praises him to Elizabeth and the Gardiners, "If I was to go through the world, I could not meet with a better. But I have always observed, that they who are good-natured when children, are good-natured when they grow up; and he was always the sweetest -tempered, most generous-hearted, boy in the world" (p 249).

This echoes the young Earl Fitzwilliam's good nature. He was sent to Eton public school at the age of eight and contemporary records from there described him as 'friendly and mild tempered, though not an academic'. A fellow pupil, Lord Carlisle, expressed his qualities in this poem.

Say will Fitzwilliam ever want a heart,
Cheerful his ready blessings to impart?
Will not another woe his bosom share,
The widow's sorrow and the orphan's prayer?
Who aids the old, who soothes the mother's cry.
Who wipes the tear from off the Virgin's eye?
Who feeds the Hungry, who assists the lame?
All, all re-echo with Fitzwilliam's name.
Thou know'st I hate to flatter, yet in thee,
No fault, my friend no single speck I see.

Mr Darcy was 'the best landlord' as was the 4th Earl Fitzwilliam.

Elizabeth and Mr and Mrs Gardiner are told by Mrs Reynolds that Mr Darcy was kind to the poor adding that "He is the best landlord, and the best master...that ever lived, not like the wild young men nowadays, who think of nothing but themselves. There is not one of his tenants or servants but what will give him a good name" (p 249).

In the real world, Earl Fitzwilliam 'Devoted...hundreds of thousands of his income to political and public causes. In return, he received affection, respect and reputation, but he never sought...financial rewards, nor honours' (*Whig Principles and Party Politics* p 386). Lord Holland wrote that the Earl had 'courage and honesty' in great situations, "The sort of importance he enjoyed for half a century ...derived from his goodness and generosity and from the combination of gentleness and courage which distinguished his amiable and unpretending character...such generosity of feeling, firmness of purpose, and tenderness of heart... commanded the affection and confidence of the public". Earl Fitzwilliam was a racehorse breeder, a great patron of the turf and at Wentworth House continued his uncle Lord Rockingham's tradition of open hospitality to the crowds which gathered for the races at York in August and Doncaster in September.

Bonds of familial love - Mr Darcy and his sister Georgiana - The Earl and his four sisters.

Mr Darcy shows a familial love and duty of care to his sister Georgiana, performed with reserve similar to that of Earl Fitzwilliam who, at twenty, was noted for the solicitous care he took of his four sisters after the death of his mother in 1769. They both had a problem aunt too. Mr Darcy's aunt, lady Catherine de Bourgh, tries to interfere when she hears rumours of his forthcoming engagement. She makes it her business to query Elizabeth Bennet's suitability as a marriage partner for her nephew. It seems beyond coincidence that Earl Fitzwilliam suffered from his aunt, the overpowering Lady Rockingham, who was known to have curbed his youthful eagerness too much, which later compromised his role in the party leadership for some years.

A taste for collecting fine art and books

In *Pride and Prejudice* Miss Bingley remarks on Mr Darcy's 'delightful library' and he tells her that "It ought to be good...It has been the work of many generations", but she compliments him with "And then you have added so much to it yourself, you are always buying books" (p 38). Similarly, after a grand tour of Europe Earl Fitzwilliam became a lifelong devotee of painting and the arts and cultivated a taste for fine books.

Jane gives Mr Darcy's relatives the names of those of the 4th Earl Fitzwilliam

In *Pride and Prejudice*, Jane Austen combines the names of two great Yorkshire families, the Earls Fitzwilliam and the D'Arcy's, Earls of Holdernesse, to create her hero Mr Darcy (Fitzwilliam Darcy). Mr Darcy's mother was Lady Anne Fitzwilliam, who married a Mr Darcy of Pemberley and became Lady Anne Darcy. She and Lady Catherine De Bourgh were sisters, and their brother the Earl was the father of Colonel Fitzwilliam "the younger son of an Earl" (p 183) and first cousin of Mr Darcy. Colonel Fitzwilliam was very central to the developments at Rosins with Elizabeth Bennet and Mr Darcy.

In real life, the 4th Earl was the son of the 3rd Earl Fitzwilliam and Lady Anne Watson Wentworth who was the sister of the Marquis of Rockingham. The Marquis was head of the Whig Aristocracy and Prime Minister of Great Britain from 1765 to 1766 and again in 1782. Rockingham died without an heir in July of that year and the Earl inherited his uncle's large estates in England and in Ireland. So the 4th Earl Fitzwilliam was the first heir to the combined Fitzwilliam Wentworth family fortune, and was also known as 4th Earl Fitzwilliam Wentworth.

But there are more names to add. The 3rd Earl Fitzwilliam was also the last Earl of Holderness, whose name was Robert D'Arcy. So the 4th Earl Fitzwilliam had the name D'Arcy Fitzwilliam on his father's side and the name Wentworth on his mother's side.

The ancestral tree of the Fitzwilliams

The 4th Earl Fitzwilliam had a distinguished heritage and was said to be descended from William the Conqueror. In the 16th century, Sir William Fitzwilliam was appointed Lord Justice of Ireland and also held the lease of Fotheringay Castle at the time when Mary Queen of Scots was executed there. The Earl's ancestors, the D'Arcys also had held office in Ireland and were related by marriage to the De Burgh family who were Earls of Ulster. The titles of the Barony of D'Arcy were linked to the Earldom of Holderness, which held land in Yorkshire with Hornby Castle one of its residences. Robert D'Arcy (1718-1778) was the last Earl of Holderness. He left no sons so his title became extinct. The Duke of Newcastle wrote of him "He is very diligent and exact in all his proceedings. He has great temper mixed with proper resolution. He has no pride about him, though a D'Arcy". One particularly distinguished ancestor a Lord Darcy held religious convictions which led him to support Catherine of Aragon, declaring his person and goods were at the King's disposal but as to matrimonial causes he had always understood that they were spiritual and belonged to ecclesiastical jurisdiction. He was later implicated in the Pilgrimage of Grace (Rising in Yorkshire in 1536 against King Henry VIII's break with the Catholic Church) which led to his beheading on the 30th June 1537 and his body lies with other D'Arcys in the Church of St. Botolph in London. But sadly, in the 20th Century, the Fitzwilliam line finished when the title became extinct upon the death of the 10th Earl, William Thomas George Wentworth-Fitzwilliam, in 1979.

Watson, Wentworth and Woodhouse

Many of Jane's characters in her novels have the three titled family names of the Marquis of Rockingham, Watson (*The Watsons*, unfinished), Woodhouse (*Emma*) and Wentworth (*Persuasion*). Thomas Wentworth the first Earl of Strafford practised religious tolerance to the Irish Catholics. Such empathy showed a sense of family connection by Jane because her mother's family tree had a Wentworth connection. These are names associated with the nobility of this one family whose lineage stretches back hundreds of years. They are Jane Austen's Family names too which held a resonance for her and she was proud of her family. To quote D. McAteer 'Shake her mother's family tree and out fall forebears whose names were - Wentworth, Woodhouse, Churchill, Willoughby, de Bourgh, D'Arcy, Fitzwilliam, Gardiner, Watson, Middleton, Tilney, Brandon, Gre(n)ville, Bertram, Ferrars, Dashwood, Elliot, Musgrave, Bingley, Bennet, and Dudley'.

Jane clearly had a prevailing interest and romantic attachment to such personal family links, to history and social position. This history had initial links with Ireland too. Illustrious names veiled with the romance of history, which become vibrantly alive once again on the page under Jane's pen. Their significance can conjure up an aura and evoke rich associations from the past, supplying useful detail and interest to embellish her creations. Even though his lineage ended with the death of the 10th Earl Fitzwilliam, the legacy of the "good man" lives on in the character of Mr Darcy of *Pride and Prejudice*.

CHAPTER 7

A CAFÉ IN EDGEWORTHSTOWN

I fulfilled a promise to visit Maria Edgeworth's home in County Longford, curious to see where she lived her extraordinary life. This time I was alone as I travelled through the centre of Ireland, changed trains at Athlone and arrived in Edgeworthstown on a lovely sunny afternoon. Stopping to eat at the first cafe I saw, I wondered why the men were staring at me. On leaving I saw lots of trucks parked around and realized I had entered a truck driver's cafe. I booked into a hotel for the night and next morning I walked across a field to Edgeworth house. A woman answered the door and I said to her "I'd like to see where Maria Edgeworth lived". She told me that the house was now a nursing home but invited me into a lovely spacious room with a very high ceiling. As I looked up to my right there on the wall was a huge mural in beautiful colours, one I had seen in many books. It was of Maria and her father sitting at opposite ends of a very long table, with lots of children gathered around at either side. Richard Edgeworth looked dignified and intelligent, while Maria's lovely face was framed in long fair curls and a hat with trailing ribbons. The mural, over 200 years old encapsulated this extraordinary family learning together, and I wished it to be there for ever. Then I was taken to a table with a glass top and saw some of the Yearly Reviews of the Edgeworth Society. In a kind of dream, I thanked the women and returned to town. On my way, I spotted a plaque on the side of a shed-like building which informed that Richard Edgeworth opened his school here in 1816. I felt privileged to have seen this visual reminder of Richard and Maria's passion for education.

'The Great Maria' Jane's literary companion

Jane Austen and Maria Edgeworth attained true greatness in their writing and Jane had a literary affinity with Maria whose fiction, had brought a sense of excitement into her life. From 1795 Maria became Jane's literary companion. Her writings, principally *Letters for Literary Ladies*, her 'Tale' *Belinda* and her *Essays on Practical Education* inspired Jane.

Writing to her niece in 1814, Jane summed up her gratitude to Maria, "My Dear Anna... Walter Scott has no business to write novels, especially good ones. - It is not fair. - He has Fame and Profit enough as a Poet, and should not be taking the bread out of other people's mouths. - I do not like him, and do not mean to like Waverley if I can help it...I have made up my mind to like no Novels really, but Miss Edgeworth's, Yours, and my own" (Lt 101).

The extraordinary life of Maria Edgeworth

Maria Edgeworth became one of the most celebrated female writers of the early 19th Century. She was feted as a celebrity in the literary world of London where during her short visit in 1803 she met Lord Byron and dined at the home of Lady Spencer. Her fame spread to Scotland and then to Europe and America. Born in Black Bourton, Oxfordshire in 1767, to Anne Maria and Richard Lovell Edgeworth, she was destined to have the most unusual and unconventional childhood. At the age of six her mother died and within a year her father had married again. Around this time he inherited the Edgeworth estate, with its beautiful house in Co. Longford, Ireland, and took his family to live there. From 1775, Maria was educated first at the school of Mrs Lattefiere in Derby and later at the school of Mrs Davis in Upper Wimpole Street, London. Here she excelled in French and Latin, and amused the other pupils with her storytelling. In 1782 she was brought back to Co. Longford, and lived there until her death in 1849. On her return one of her first tasks for her father was to translate Madame De Genlis's *Adele et Theodore* into English. Later Maria gave French titles to some of her stories and French phrases are sprinkled throughout them.

Maria had a remarkable relationship with the one 'constant' adult in her life, her father. By his side, she learned estate management and became familiar with the customs and culture of Irish country life at every level. She travelled around the estate on a donkey, mixing with the workers and tenants, both Catholic and Protestant, and learned all sorts of trades used in building and farming. By the year 1798 her father had married his fourth wife, Frances Anne Beaufort. Maria, at the age of 31, was having to participate in the education of her 'twenty brothers and sisters, whom she was never happy away from'. She became a brilliant tutor to them and at the same time gained ideas for her wonderful stories for young adults. They were published from 1795 onwards and were some of the first realistic fiction ever written for this age group, brimming with facts about science, travel, geography and history. Among their cheerfulness, humour and sense, Maria had a common theme of teaching the child to think for itself.

The young Maria mixed with the aristocrats of the area, she wrote of the Longfords of Pakenham Hall, where during 'long tedious dinners…everyone ate and drank to excess…the conversation of men dealt…with horses and dogs and that of the ladies with dress and scandal'. In 1783 her report of a Harper's festival held in the market town of Granard was published in the local newspaper. The diversity and uniqueness of Maria's life was experience for her later sophisticated society 'novels'.

Maria's rise to fame

In 1795 *Letters for Literary Ladies* was published followed by:

The Parent's Assistant - 1796
Essays on Practical Education - 1798
Castle Rackrent - 1800
Belinda - 1801
Essay on Irish Bulls - 1802
Popular Tales - 1804
Moral Tales for Young People - 1805
Leonore – 1806

Tales of Fashionable Life - 1809 and 1812 of which one of its stories, *The Absentee*, was a monumental success. It was published in America and then France in 1813. Back in Edgeworth House, Maria and her father revamped it for the stage and sent it to Sheridan in London, but the Lord Chamberlain would not grant it a license, due to the current state of things in Ireland.

Maria revisited London in 1813 and in one of her letters describes the comfort of the mail coach from Holyhead to London. By now she had reached the height of her fame. Another young lady, Jane Austen, was also in London having had two novels published anonymously, *Sense and Sensibility* (1811) and *Pride and Prejudice* (1813).

Jane's literary journey.

G.K. Chesterton wrote that 'A Writer's credit card is his childhood' and this statement is true for both Maria Edgeworth and Jane Austen. They both had a talent for writing from a young age. They both attended school for a time during their childhood. Jane and her older sister Cassandra spent two short spells at school before returning to Steventon, their schooldays over. Between 1795 and 1800 Jane had written the first drafts of three of her novels, *Sense and Sensibility*, *Pride and Prejudice* and *Northanger Abbey*. In 1797 her father, the Rev. George Austen, offered to pay a London company, Thomas Cadell, to publish *Pride and Prejudice* (then *First Impressions*) but his request was declined. In 1801 the family moved to Bath. In 1803, R. Crosby, a London publisher, paid ten pounds for Susan (later called *Northanger Abbey*). Jane's father died in 1805 before any of her novels were published. In 1809, after a spell living in Southampton, the family went to live at Chawton, Hampshire.

Jane was happy to be back in the countryside of her youth and she was soon 'lopping and cropping' *Sense and Sensibility* which was anonymously published in October 1811 'By a Lady' two months before her 36th birthday. Princess Charlotte, the daughter of the Prince Regent loved it. The Aristocracy loved it. Lady Bessborough, friend of Richard Sheridan 'thought it was a clever novel' (M. Laski p 80) and Charles Fox's nephew told Charles Austen that he enjoyed it. (C. Tomalin p 220).

In January 1813, *Pride and Prejudice* was published this time 'By a Lady, Author of *Sense and Sensibility*' to instant acclaim. Its heroine, Elizabeth Bennet, became a favourite with readers. Jane wrote to Cassandra that *Pride and Prejudice* was "too light, and bright, and sparkling; it wants shade; it wants…a long chapter of sense…if not, of solemn specious nonsense, about something unconnected with the story…a critique on Walter Scott, or the history of Bonaparte" (Lt 77).

Jane was now enjoying her success as she drove around London in her brother Henry's Barouche visiting the Somerset House exhibitions and Pall Mall. At an exhibition in Spring Gardens, Chelsea, *Pride and Prejudice* was on her mind as she looked for 'portraits' of Mrs Bingley and Mrs Darcy. She reveals her personality a little when she writes to Cassandra defending her fear of being introduced to a Miss Burdett conceding "If I am a wild Beast, I cannot help it. It is not my own fault" (Lt 80-1813).

Jane sends a copy of *Emma* to Maria Edgeworth but Maria did not acknowledge it

In May 1814 Jane's third novel *Mansfield Park* was published. She completed her fourth novel, *Emma,* in March 1815 and John Murray (Lord Byron's publisher) agreed to publish it. Both novels were once again published anonymously by 'By a Lady'. Jane was staying in London with her brother Henry who became very ill with a fever. Cassandra, James and Edward came quickly to London where, after weeks of anxiety, Henry recovered. His physician a Dr Baillie told Jane that the Prince Regent admired her novels and kept a set in each of his residences. She was invited on a tour of the exquisite Carlton House palace and its library by Mr Clarke the librarian. After discussions with Cassandra and Henry Jane agreed to dedicate *Emma* to the Prince, and had a set bound in gold and scarlet with the Prince of Wales feathers on the spine, sent to Mr. Clarke. In December 1815, the Morning Post announced the publication of *Emma*. This was the last of her novels Jane saw in print, and astonishingly she sent a copy to Maria Edgeworth. Was this gratitude on Jane's part? or was she trying to communicate, to make contact with Maria. The sad outcome was Maria did not reply to Jane's friendly gesture. In the year 1816 *Emma* was published in France and America. Jane by now very ill, continued to write and began *Sanditon* in which she was heralding the age of the great British seaside.

Jane departed this life on the 18th of July 1817 and her novels *Northanger Abbey* and *Persuasion* were published the following year. In *Northanger Abbey* Jane defends novel writing and names Maria's *Belinda* as deserving of the highest praise (NA pp 37/38). But as shall be revealed later it is *Persuasion* that Maria Edgeworth had a real affection for.

There is no evidence of Maria and Jane having ever met.

Yet their paths may have crossed because from 1766 Maria Edgeworth's father Richard Lovell Edgeworth had a house in the village of Hare Hatch, Berkshire, where Jane's aunt and uncle Mr and Mrs Leigh-Perrot lived. Jane and Cassandra would be invited to stay with this couple sometimes. On occasions Mr Leigh-Perrot helped with Richard's scientific experiments, one being the telegraphing from Hare Hatch to Nettlebed by means of windmills. In 1799 Mrs Leigh Perrot was accused of shoplifting in Bath and was imprisoned for seven months. When she was eventually acquitted, Maria Edgeworth's father sent a flattering letter of congratulation from Ireland. "I do not think that I ever felt so much astonishment or indignation…Among my numerous friends and acquaintance if there was a couple whom I could have selected as the farthest removed from being the objects of such a villainous attack it would have been yourselves! I trouble you, my Dear Sir, with a few lines to express the deep sense that I have of regard and esteem for you and the amiable partner of your happiness, for so many as thirty-four years we have been acquainted, and during that time I do not think that I have met any man of such singularly nice feelings of honour and justice…with tears in my eyes I write to you' (Chris Viveash p 165).

Maria's writings influenced Jane Austen's novels

A short story from Maria's first published work *Letters for Literary Ladies* (1795) furnished Jane with a plan for her first novel *Sense and Sensibility* which she began about this time. Walton Litz in his book Jane Austen: A Study of Her Artistic Development suggested that Jane conceived the idea for her novel *Sense and Sensibility* from *Letters of Julia and Caroline* one of the stories from *Letters for Literary Ladies*. Maria's story (in complete form at the close of this chapter) is about two young friends Caroline and Julia. Caroline is in control of her feelings and guided by her common sense, and Julia's extremes of feeling and passion rule her behaviour, guide her morality and in the end, destroy her.

In *Sense and Sensibility* Jane Austen gives the characteristics of Caroline to Elinor and those of Julia to Marianne. Caroline and Elinor are rational, Julia and Marianne are irrational. Jane was aware of the fate that befell Maria Edgeworth's Julia but she intended her Marianne to live although Willoughby deserts her. Marianne is supported by Elinor and her mother and in time goes through a kind of metamorphosis emerging healed in soul and body. In due course, she marries Colonel Brandon. Maria Edgeworth did not intend to rescue her Julia, making her an example of what could happen to 'Literary Ladies' if they strayed. Julia is vulnerable. Unless she meets with a man who can accept her extremes of feeling and passion she is heading for a downfall. Her marriage to a Lord is short. She loses her respect and moves to France 'reduced to absolute want in a foreign country without friend or foe'. Eventually, near death, she returns to England. She sends for Caroline. Later Caroline comments 'by fatal imprudence...all her great, and good and amiable qualities were...lost to the world and to herself' (*Letters of Julia and Caroline*).

Jane Austen sets her character, Marianne, on a path of salvation. It is as if Jane is having a dialogue with Maria Edgeworth, as she presents a similar argument and circumstance, but whereas Maria tends to preach and scold in an exposure of action, Jane Austen imbues the situation with vitality, humour and discrete observation. Through the trials of Marianne and Elinor we experience not only the whims of passion and the diversity of human behaviour, but also the consolation of redemption and a happy ending.

In *Sense and Sensibility* Elinor possessed, 'a strength of understanding and coolness of judgement, which qualified her, though only nineteen, to be the counsellor of her mother and...counteract...that eagerness of mind in Mrs Dashwood which...led to imprudence. Elinor had an excellent heart...and her feelings were strong; but she knew how to govern them: it was a knowledge which her mother had yet to learn and which one of her sisters had resolved never to be taught' (*SS* p 6). Elinor can be compared with Caroline who as the guide of her friend Julia, tells her "to reflect upon her feelings!".

Jane Austen writes that Marianne's abilities are 'quite equal to her sister Elinor's. She was sensible and clever; but eager in everything; her sorrows, her joys, could have no moderation. She was...everything but prudent' (*SS* p 6), which connects with Julia's statement to Caroline that "Human prudence does nothing - fortune everything". When the Dashwood family learn that they will have to quit their home, the beautiful Norland, Mrs Dashwood and Marianne 'encouraged each other...in the violence of their affliction' (*SS* p 7). Again, the words connect with Maria Edgeworth's Julia, who writes of "violent grief".

Marianne says to her mother, "I could not be happy with a man whose taste did not...coincide with my own...Oh! Mama, how spiritless...was Edward's manner in reading to us last night!" ... "Elinor has not my feeling...it would have broke my heart had I loved him, to hear him read with so little sensibility" (*SS* pp 17/18). What Marianne says supports Julia's letter where she distinguishes between both kinds of emotional natures and says "Reflect upon my feelings! Dear Caroline, is it not enough that I do feel?...You tell me that by… indulging I shall weaken my natural sensibility…I must not… indulge my taste for romance and poetry, lest I waste that sympathy on fiction which reality so much better deserves".

Maria Edgeworth's Julia and Jane Austen's Marianne are essentially selfish in that they are aware of their own feelings but not so considerate of the feelings of others. The egotistic Marianne, dismisses Brandon's apparent lack of response to her singing and playing as 'a man of five and thirty might well have outlived all acuteness of feeling' (*SS* p 35). She is like Julia who writes to Caroline "You urge me to think; I profess only to feel". Marianne can only perceive through the filter of her own self-absorbed notion of sensibility. When Willoughby makes fun of Colonel Brandon, "whom everybody speaks well of, and nobody cares about" (*SS* p 50) Elinor does not allow him to get away with his unjust remarks. Marianne chose to ignore his callousness.

Marianne falls in love with Willoughby 'His person and air were equal to...her fancy...for the hero of a favourite story' (*SS* p 43) and 'their enjoyment of dancing and music was mutual...on the subject of books...He acquiesced in all her decisions' (*SS* p 47). Unlike Maria Edgeworth, who makes her point with severe concern, Jane Austen uses humour, as Elinor tell Marianne with sarcasm "for one morning...you have done pretty well...You know what he thinks of Cowper and Scott...of his admiring Pope...Another meeting will suffice to explain his sentiments on picturesque beauty...and then you can have nothing farther to ask" (*SS* p 47). Soon Willoughby deserts Marianne who appears inconsolable but Jane Austen undercuts her emotionalism with more humour 'Such violence of affliction...could not be supported for ever; it sunk within a few days into a calmer melancholy' (*SS* pp 83/84).

There are many direct similarities in the texts of both Jane and Maria. Mrs Dashwood, when faced with the possibility of Marianne's demise can change to be 'calm' (*SS* p 334), the qualities which Julia applied to Caroline, mentioning "calm happiness" in the letter. Again, Elinor has fears for Marianne that "Her systems have all the…tendency of setting propriety at nought" (*SS* p 56). The concept of 'system' is also in Julia's letter as she writes to Caroline "I have no system! that is the very difference between us…how vain are systems".

Elinor loves Edward and is shocked on hearing of Lucy Steele's secret engagement to him. She 'concealed an emotion and distress beyond anything she had ever felt before' (*SS* p 135) and 'was stronger alone and her own good sense so well supported her' (*SS* p 141). This illustrates in practice what Maria Edgeworth's Caroline writes "the even temper…virtue without heroism".

At Lady Middleton's party as they see Willoughby, Elinor says to Marianne not to "betray what you feel to everybody present" (*SS* p 176). When Marianne shows 'a torrent of unresisted grief' Elinor tries to provide an altruistic side "Exert yourself, dear Marianne…if you would not kill yourself and all who love you. Think of your mother". Marianne replies "Elinor, you cannot have an idea of what I suffer" (*SS* p 185), but Elinor keeps silent about her own unhappiness. Later when she must reveal to Marianne, Edward's engagement to Lucy Steele it was 'not accompanied by violent agitation, nor impetuous grief' (*SS* p 261). She exclaims to Marianne "If you can think me capable of ever feeling - surely you may suppose that I have suffered now" (*SS* p 264). Through Elinor's suffering, Jane Austen reveals that appearances can courageously and unselfishly conceal real emotion and hurt.

When Marianne dismisses Mrs Jennings as incapable of feeling, she forgets that she came to London at the invitation of Mrs Jennings in the hope of seeing Willoughby. Jane Austen points to Marianne's self-obsession. During the three-day journey to London Marianne spoke only to admire the scenery. It was Elinor who 'behaved with the greatest attention to Mrs Jennings, talked with her, laughed with her' (*SS* p 160).

Jane also expresses and underpins a Christian perspective to her moral conclusion. She gives Marianne the opportunity to make amends. Marianne tells Elinor, "My illness has made me think...Had I died - it would have been self-destruction. I did not know my danger till the danger was removed...I wonder...that the very eagerness of my desire to live, to have time for atonement to my God, and to you all, did not kill me at once. Had I died, - in what peculiar misery should I have left you, my nurse, my friend, my sister! ...How should I have lived in your remembrance! - My mother too...The kindness...of Mrs Jennings, I had repaid with ungrateful contempt...and if I do mix in other society it will be only to shew that my spirit is humbled, my heart amended, and that I can practise the civilities, the lesser duties of life, with gentleness, and forbearance" (*SS* pp 345-347). Maria Edgeworth's story sadly concludes with the dying Julia saying to Caroline "Your kindness touches me more than all the rest, but how ashamed you must be of such a friend! Oh, Caroline! To die a disgrace to all who ever loved me".

A very exciting time for novel writers

In the latter half of the 18th Century the novel was emerging in all its diversity. Women began to write novels some of whom were Charlotte Lennox (*The Female Quixote*, 1752) - Charlotte Smith (*Emmeline*, 1785) - Mrs Radcliff (*The Mysteries of Udolpho*,1794). Circulating libraries and subscriptions to mailing lists were features of town and country. Jane Austen was on a mailing list and so was Maria Edgeworth in Ireland. Early in 1800 public opinion was divided as to the merits of the novel and many saw the novel as having too great an emotional effect on people. The poet Crabbe wrote that 'novels had meant too much to him in his starved youth' and Cowper attacked the 'immoral persuasion of the popular novel.'

Maria Edgeworth wanted her books classed as 'moral tales'. She makes this clear in her preface to *Belinda* "Every Author has a right to give what appellation he may think proper to his works. The public have also a right to accept or refuse the classification that is presented. The following work is offered as a Moral Tale - the author not wishing to acknowledge a Novel...so much folly, error and vice are disseminated in books classed under this denomination, that it is hoped the wish to assume another title will be attributed to feelings that are laudable, and not fastidious" (April 20th 1801).

On the other hand, Jane was passionate about the novel and wrote in one of her letters that she and her family were all great novel readers and proud of it. I discovered that in *Northanger Abbey* she sang the praises of Maria Edgeworth's 'Moral Tale' *Belinda* calling it a novel of wit and genius. She writes 'Although our productions have afforded more extensive and unaffected pleasure...no species of composition had been so much decried. From pride, ignorance, or fashion, our foes are almost as many as our readers...there seems almost a general wish of...undervaluing the labour of the novelist, and of slighting the performances which have only genius, wit, and taste to recommend them... "And what are you reading, Miss?" - "Oh! It is only a novel!" replies the young lady; while she lays down her book with affected indifference or momentary shame. - "It is only Cecilia, or Camilla, or Belinda;" or in short, only some work in which the greatest powers of the mind are displayed...the liveliest effusions of wit and humour are conveyed to the world in the best-chosen language' (*NA* pp 37/38).

By the year 1813 three women, Fanny Burney, Maria, and Jane herself had raised the society novel to near perfection. Its development and progression can be traced from Fanny Burney's Camilla to Maria's *Belinda* and to Jane's *Pride and Prejudice*. Maria was thirty-three when her *Belinda* was published in 1801, and Jane at nearly twenty-six, was over ten years away from her first publication. Henry Austen wrote after Jane's death that he would not be surprised 'if one day her work would rank up there with a D'Arblay (Fanny Burney's married name) or an Edgeworth'. Henry's prediction was too modest, as neither Fanny Burney's nor Maria's work are well known today, but his sister's fame two centuries later is boundless.

Belinda

Belinda was Maria Edgeworth's most successful novel and when it was published in 1801 it was hailed as a benchmark in novel writing. It had many firsts in its composition. It is a tale of love and marriage intertwined with themes integral to Maria's vision for society concerning education, responsibility and sound moral values. It is enthralling and reflects Maria's knowledge of subjects, from Confucius to the Classics, to macaws and goldfish. Society is reproduced in all classes including a specific mimicry of a West Indian dialect for the black servants who have their own identity and concerns. Maria had the courage to introduce issues such as the slave trade and the education of women. She refers to the kept mistress, and scheming disloyal wife as a foil to emphasize the joys of a virtuous and happy marriage. Men are depicted as needing the correct educational grounding to achieve, avoid vice and contribute to society. More sinister and neglected aspects of society are touched on, like the effects of unrestricted use of opium, the lure and power of gambling and the problem of drinking.

Belinda opens and concludes with theatrical imagery highlighting the interplay between appearance and reality, as a perilous pathway between truth and deceit through which the heroine, *Belinda*, finds her way to determine her true love. Her idealistic virtues impress Lady Delacour, a female rake, who is reformed through contact with her. Lady Delacour, in my opinion, one of the best characters in fiction, supplies much of the wit and livelier interest to the plot, 'Abroad, and at home Lady Delacour was two different persons. Abroad she appeared all life, spirit, and good humour - at home, listless, fretful and melancholy; she seemed like a spoiled actress of the stage, over stimulated by applause, and exhausted by the exertions of supporting fictitious character. When her house was filled with well-dressed crowds, when it blazed with lights, and resounded with music and dancing, Lady Delacour...shone the soul and spirit of pleasure and frolic. But the moment the company retired, when the music ceased, and the lights were extinguishing, the spell was dissolved' (*Belinda* p11).

Belinda closes with a tableau staged by Lady Delacour, who stresses the roles each character has played in the story. As she addresses the audience she says "Our tale contains a moral...You all have wit enough to find it out" (*Belinda* p 478).

One of the funniest episodes in *Belinda* is a duel between women dressed as men, where the machinations of cross dressing fuel the plot. Maria shows her brilliance for tragi- comedy as Lady Delacour tells her story of when she was canvassing for an election and her rival Mrs Luttridge annoys her by ordering panniers (baskets) full of election favours twice as large as her own. Lady Delacour retaliates with a caricature The Ass and Her panniers. Mrs Luttridge's is buoyed up by Harriet Freke a mischief maker, who encourages the two ladies to fight a duel. Lady Delacour is petrified, having never fired a pistol in her life, but Harriet urges 'honour before blood'. At that moment, Mrs Luttridge discovers a whitlow on her hand and cannot 'draw the trigger' so to satisfy honour they fire harmlessly in the air but Lady Delacour's pistol recoils and damages her breast. Crowds gather on hearing the shots and are scandalised to see women duelling in men's clothing and set about ducking them in the pond. Clarence Hervey appears on the scene and rescues the women. At the same time, he loses a bet with a Frenchman, about a race between turkeys and pigs and which would reach the market first. Here Maria paints a farcical scene of broad humour with squeaking, grunting pigs and gobbling turkeys which make possible the ladies escape from the mob. Their husbands lose the election because of their behaviour, and victory is awarded to a man "whose wife...was a proper behaved woman".

If *Belinda* has faults it is that at times the plot is lost in Maria's astounding range of detail. She also lacked a self-aware critical perspective. Jane recognised these errors and discreetly avoids them, concentrating on a more carefully honed sphere of activity in her family assemblages.

Jane Austen obviously loved *Belinda* and was inspired by it.

Finding the ideal man is implicit in Maria's *Belinda*. Mrs Stanhope, a notorious matchmaker has already 'settled five nieces' and has the rich Sir Philip Baddely in mind for *Belinda* who refuses him "Of his character temper, and manners, I know enough to be convinced, that our union could...make us both miserable". Mrs Stanhope angry with *Belinda* tells her "Refuse whom you please - go where you please...manage for yourself as you please" (*Belinda* pp 214/5). In *Pride and Prejudice*, Mrs Bennet has five daughters and the 'business of her life' is to get them married. She wants Elizabeth to marry Mr Collins, but when he pops the question Elizabeth replies "I am perfectly serious in my refusal - You could not make me happy, and I am convinced that I am the last woman in the world who would make you so" (*PP* p 107). Mrs Bennet's anger is equally like Mrs Stanhope's as she confronts Elizabeth, "I do not know who is to maintain you when your father is dead...I have done with you from this very day" (*PP* p 113).

When the romantic hero Clarence Hervey is introduced to Belinda he is dubious "of one of the Stanhope school...*Belinda* Portman is a composition of art and affectation" (*Belinda* p 26). This resembles the wealthy Darcy's prejudice towards Elizabeth's family as he says to her "Could you expect me to rejoice in the inferiority of your connections...whose condition in life is so decidedly beneath my own?" (*PP* p 192). When *Belinda* is told, "a heart such as yours is formed for love in its highest purest, happiest state" she replies that this can only happen "with a man of sense and virtue" (*Belinda* p 360). This reflects Elizabeth's feelings about Darcy "I love him. Indeed he has no improper pride. He is perfectly amiable" (*PP* p 376).

Rousseau's concept of the innocent boy in *Emile* (1762) is used by Maria and Jane

Maria Edgeworth uses Rousseau's concept of innocence in *Belinda* and Jane Austen also uses this concept in *Sense and Sensibility* and *Emma*. In *Belinda* Clarence Hervey revolted by the immorality about him decides to find an innocent girl for his wife. In the New Forest, he meets 'this child of nature' 17-year-old Rachel who he calls Virginia. He is charmed when she chooses 'a moss rose bud over a pair of diamond earrings' (p 371). However, on meeting *Belinda* again, he discerns that she, 'could be a companion...to him for life... Virginia would merely be his pupil, or his plaything...The virtues of Virginia sprang from sentiment; those of *Belinda* from reason' (p 379). In *Sense and Sensibility*, the young Eliza was seduced by Willoughby and left "in a situation of the utmost distress...He neither returned, nor wrote" (*SS* p 209). Then in *Emma* the naive Harriet is "the natural daughter of nobody knows whom...taught nothing useful...too young and too simple to have acquired anything herself" (*E* p 61).

Maria's passion was education

Maria's theories from *Essays on Practical Education* (1798) are traceable in Jane's novels *Mansfield Park* and *Emma*. Maria had a passion for education and saw school as an adventure, writing 'All the world is a school; and men and women merely pupils'. She considered love, understanding of the child's natural impulses, and freedom, together with the practical approach to learning, a successful method in educating children. Surrounded by the children of her father's four marriages she became an expert. Her books were text-books for a school of life with its three stages: childhood, youth and adulthood.

Essays on Practical Education was first published in 1798 and it covered every aspect of education. It was considered to be a century before its time. At this stage in the growth of a national education system, Maria and her father were years ahead in the education debate, even before the first local school board was set up. The 'Essays' covered both abstract and practical doctrines. In the preface of the 1809 edition Richard Lovell Edgeworth writes; 'What we feel, and see, and hear and read, affects our conduct from the moment when we begin, till the moment when we cease to think. It has, therefore been my daughter's aim to promote...the progress of Education, from cradle to grave'.

'It is not sufficient in Education to store up knowledge; it is essential to arrange facts...as materials for the imagination, or the judgement to select and combine. The power of retentive memory is exercised too much, the faculty of recollective memory is exercised too little...While children are reading the history of kings, and battles, and victories, whilst they are learning tables of chronology and lessons of geography by rote, their inventive and their reasoning faculties are absolutely passive; nor are any of the facts which they learn in this manner associated with circumstances in real life...pointing out...places...in a map... knowing the latitude and longitude of all the capital cities in Europe...are not the tests of a good education. We should rather, if we were to examine a boy of ten years old...produce proofs of his being able to reason accurately; of his quickness in invention, of his habits of industry and application, of his having learned to generalize his ideas and to apply his observations and his principles; if we found that he had learned...any of these things, we should be in little pain about grammar, or geography'.

The bravura of Maria's theories and ideas were adopted by Jane who in the most naturalistic manner wove them into *Mansfield Park* and *Emma*. It is likely that they occupied her thinking on occasions at Chawton, when some of her twenty-four nieces and nephews came to stay.

In *Mansfield Park*, nine-year-old Fanny Price is brought from her deprived home in Portsmouth to live with the wealthy Sir Thomas Bertram and his family at their large estate. 'Fanny could read, work, and write' (*MP* p 18) but she had been taught nothing more. Her cousins, Maria and Julia Bertram, thought she was ignorant, "Dear Mamma, only think, my cousin cannot put the map of Europe together...cannot tell the principal rivers in Russia...she never heard of Asia Minor...she does not know the difference between watercolours and crayons!...Did you ever hear anything so stupid?...I should have been ashamed...if I had not known better long before I was so old as she is...How long ago it is, aunt, since we used to repeat the chronological order of the kings of England...the principal events of their reigns !". The other sister added "and of the Roman emperors as low as Severus...the Heathen Mythology ...all the Metals...Planets, and distinguished philosophers". Her aunt Mrs Norris answered "Very true...my dears, but you are blessed with wonderful memories...your poor cousin has probably none at all...you must make allowance...and pity her deficiency" (*MP* pp18/19).

Maria Bertram and her sister Julia are products of rote learning, but 'entirely deficient in the acquirements of self-knowledge, generosity, and humility' (*MP* p 19) whereas Fanny has been educated like the ideal as prescribed by Maria Edgeworth, having self-knowledge, and the ability to reason. The Bertram sisters are accomplished, but 'that...active principle, had been wanting...they had never been properly taught to govern their inclinations and tempers' (*MP* p 463). So they became victims of their education.

Also in *Essays on Practical Education* Maria and her father agree that 'A governess is no longer treated as an upper servant...she is now treated as the friend and companion of the family, and she must...have warm and permanent interest in its prosperity'. In *Emma,* Jane Austen creates Miss Taylor as such a governess for Emma Woodhouse. Miss Taylor had come to Hartfield after the death of Emma's mother and 'had fallen little short of a mother in affection...less as a governess than a friend...the affection of sixteen years...she had taught and...played with her from five years old...nursed her through the various illnesses of childhood' (*E* pp 5/6). Yet Jane Austen adds a little warning that Miss Taylor's mild temper exercised little restraint on Emma 'living together as friend and friend' (*E* p 5) and consequently Emma had too much of her own way and thought too well of herself.

Again, Jane expands on Maria's theory and touches on the

predicament of governesses in contemporary times as Jane Fairfax, only too aware of her own possible fate discuss their situation, "There are places in town...where inquiry would soon produce something - Offices for the sale - not quite of human flesh - but of human intellect" (*E* p 300).

Maria's letters reveal that she read Jane's novels.

Although Jane did not get a response from Maria on sending her a copy of *Emma* it would have delighted her to know the Maria read her novels and commented on five of them. First is *Pride and Prejudice*. In May 1813 while on a journey from Cambridge, Maria writes to her brother "Now we are again on the London Rd., and nothing interrupted our perusal of P/P...I am desired not to give you my opinion...but desire you to get it...I cannot comment until I see Mr B". This letter is puzzling and Mr B remains a mystery.

Second is *Mansfield Park*. She writes to her cousin in 1814, "We have been much entertained with *Mansfield Park*".

Third is *Emma*. In January 1816, she wrote to her brother "The Authoress of '*Pride and Prejudice*' has been so good as to send me a new novel just published, *Emma*...There was no story in it...Miss Emma found that the man whom she designed for Harriet's lover was an admirer of her own". Maria was not at all appreciative of *Emma*.

Fourth is *Northanger Abbey* and Maria writes to her aunt Mrs Ruxton (Chosen Letters) that General Tilney's behaviour "is quite out of drawing and out of nature". That was all, nothing about the passage which praised her own novel *Belinda*.

Fifth is *Persuasion* and Maria clearly had a high regard for this novel writing to her aunt with sensitivity and feeling "Anne and her lover...The love and lover admirably well-drawn: don't you see Captain Wentworth or rather don't you in her place feel him taking the boisterous child off her back as she kneels by the sick boy on the sofa? And is not the first meeting after their long separation admirably well done?...But I must stop, we have got no further than the disaster of Miss Musgrove jumping off the steps". (Hubbard – *Jane Austen and the Navy*) So Jane's tender writing on love in *Persuasion* won over Maria's heart.

Maria's gem *Castle Rackrent* (1800)

This chapter would not be complete without mentioning, what is considered Maria's gem, *Castle Rackrent* which was hailed a literary milestone when it was published in 1800. It is a triumph that is still largely unknown. Authors of the historical novel including Herbert Butterfield, (*The Historical Novel*, 1924) and Georg Lukacs (*The Historical Novel* 1962) fail to mention Maria Edgeworth at all.

She wrote it while her father was away courting his fourth wife Frances Beaufort. In its preface, Maria reveals a love of truth, "We cannot judge either of the feelings or of the characters of men…from their actions or their appearance…it is from their careless conversations, their half-finished sentences that we may hope…to discover their real characters". These were motivational words, and Maria's mastery of colloquial speech, conjured up the appearance of authenticity, whether or not it truly reflected the voice of a people. Much later in life, she acknowledged that, "The only character drawn from life in *Castle Rackrent* is Thady himself, the teller of the story. He was an old steward. I heard him when I first came to Ireland, and his dialect struck me, and his character; and I became so acquainted with it I began to write a family history as Thady would tell it, he seemed to stand beside me and dictate; and I wrote as fast as my pen could go, the characters all imaginary" (preface).

Maria accurately portrayed the spirit of a way of life that even as she wrote it, was becoming submerged by contemporary upheavals. It is her only novel written in an Irish regional dialect and readers, including King George III mistook it for a real account.

The idiosyncratic Thady Quirk observes and comments on his experiences in service to four generations of the Rackrent family. Each of its main characters are obsessive; Sir Patrick with drink, Sir Murtagh with the law, Sir Kit with gambling and Sir Condy with the spendthrift life of politics. The story, full of humour is enriched by a speech pattern and rhythm, reflecting its roots in the Irish language. *Castle Rackrent* honours native wit, custom and the seduction of cadence. It was an immediate success in 1800 and was a profound inspiration in the search for realism and "truth" by the great 19th century writers. The Russian author Turgenev (1818-1883 first novel *Sportsman's Sketches*, 1852) declared, "If Maria Edgeworth had not written about the poor Irish of the county Longford and the squires and squireens, it would not have occurred to me to give a literary form to my impressions about the parallel class to them in Russia". Walter Scott also paid tribute to Maria in the first of his regional novels *Waverley* (1814, Preface) which he hoped "would in some distant degree emulate the admirable Irish Portraits drawn by Miss Edgeworth".

One of her other works which brought her much fame was *Essay on Irish Bulls* (1802). It celebrates Irish humour, jokes, stories of Irish blunders, which are never blunders of the heart, according to Maria and her father, who considered themselves well informed to comment on the Irish psyche, its culture and eloquence of speech and wit. Essentially Maria, not intending to offend, was writing from her own level in society with its inevitable arrogance. But those on the receiving end might be offended. On balance, she does comment on blunders other countries can also make.

Bringing Maria and Jane together

The intriguing thing about Maria and Jane was that both had affectionate and loving fathers who encouraged their daughters in their literary pursuits.

Maria was very pretty, with long fair curly hair. She had great expression in her eyes and 'a more resigned and contemplative gaze on the world'. Small and petite, Maria was said to be shy and timid. Apparently, disliking personal compliments, she loved to hear her family complimented (*Chosen Letters*). She travelled with her father to places in Ireland, England and Europe and her letters are full of enthusiasm and joy on meeting the intellectuals and literary scholars of London and Paris. Both women never married and like Jane, Maria did fall in love. On her first trip to Paris in 1802 Maria met a Swedish diplomat Count Edelcrantz and they fell in love. Her father encouraged the romance but when the Count proposed to her before Christmas she refused him, as she did not want to leave Ireland. She was 35 and he was 46. Maria and her father left Paris as there was a danger of war; the Treaty of Amiens (1802) was being abused by Napoleon. Later it was said that at the mention of the Count's name Maria became upset. She wrote 'Literary ladies will, I am feared be losers in love, as well as in friendship, by their superiority - Cupid is a timid, playful child, and is frightened at the helmet of Minerva'.

Like Maria Jane loved being with her family especially her sister Cassandra. Her life was less flamboyant and worldly than Maria's. She often enjoyed long visits to her brother and his family in Kent and with her sister Cassandra to their friends. She travelled with her parents, to places in the West Country, Sidmouth, Dawlish, Teignmouth and Lyme Regis. Evening parties with music and dancing was a major part of her social life.

Amazingly they both lived in the city of Bath for a time but were not very happy there. Maria wrote scathingly - "Heaven preserve me from…an amateur literary tittle tattle life at Bath…Those who have lived with real friends and superiors as I have cannot bear to live with worshippers and inferiors" (Lt). In May 1801 when Jane and her family were living in Bath she informed Cassandra of "Another stupid party last night; perhaps if larger they might be less intolerable…only just enough to make one card table, with six people to look on, & talk nonsense to each other" (Lt 36). Many of her letters were of meeting people and having tea with them. She also attended one or two concerts. Jane's father died in Bath in 1805 and her communication of the news to her brother Frank is a lovely tribute to him, "Our dear father has closed his virtuous & happy life, in a death almost as free from suffering as his Children could have wished" (Lt 40 Jan. 1805). In 1808 she reveals to Cassandra "It will be two years tomorrow since we left Bath for Clifton, with what happy feelings of Escape!" (Lt 54)

Jane and Maria were both feminists, in the best sense of the word. They believed in themselves and showed courage in their commitment to writing. Each remained in the family home, each contributing to its upkeep. They were visionaries of a kind, examples of independent women living Christian lives. Their approach to religion differed though. While Maria believed that reason and rationality lead the way, Jane had faith and trusted in God's intervention and redemption.

In *Belinda* Maria includes Chaucer's definition of the good parish priest,

> *He drew his audience upwards to the sky.*
> *He taught the Gospel rather than the law*
> *And forc'd himself to drive, but loved to draw,*
> *The tithes his parish freely paid he took;*

But never sued, or curs'd with bell and book.
Wide was his parish, not contracted close
In streets - but here and there a straggling house
Yet still he was at hand, without request,
To serve the sick, and succour the distress'd
The proud he tam'd the penitent he cheer'd
Nor to rebuke the rich offender fear'd
His preaching much, but more his practice wrought,
A living sermon of the truths he taught. (p 319)

Jane choose ordination for one of her themes in *Mansfield Park* and Edmund Bertram 'takes orders'. Of the several clergymen in her novels he is the most Christ like. His reply to Mary Crawford's demeaning remark reveals his belief, "A clergyman cannot be high in state or fashion. He must not head mobs, or set the ton in dress. But I cannot call that situation nothing, which has the charge of all that is of the first importance to mankind, individually or collectively considered, temporally and eternally - which has the guardianship of religion and morals...No one here can call the office nothing. If the man who holds it is so, it is by the neglect of his duty, by forgoing its just importance, and stepping out of his place to appear what he ought not to appear" (*MP* p 92).

A sign of the times - Members of both their families caught up in The French Revolution

Relatives of both Maria and Jane were caught up in The French Revolution (1789). Father Henry Essex Edgeworth, a priest in Paris was a cousin of Maria's. In 1793 he was asked to accompany King Louis XVI to the scaffold. He stayed by the king's side until the execution was over and then made his escape to England. He returned to serve the French Royal House and died helping French prisoners of war in Latvia in 1807.

Jane's cousin, the beautiful, educated Eliza Hancock was born in 1761 in India, and at fifteen went to live in Paris along with her mother where she mixed in high society. In a letter, she describes a ball she attended, where she saw Maria Antoinette in a costume covered in diamonds and jewels, with feathers, flowers, and silver gauze. Eliza became the wife of a Count de Feuillide in 1781, and at the age of 25 gave birth to a son in London where Jane and her family visited her. Jane adored Eliza who like herself was fond of reading, dancing and music. In the Christmas of 1787 Eliza was invited to Steventon and was the star of the amateur dramatics. In 1791 Eliza and her mother narrowly avoided arrest in France by Eliza speaking fluent French then making a getaway to England. Alas the Count was guillotined in Paris in February 1794.

Richard Lovell Edgeworth - Maria's celebrated father

Maria would not have attained the fame she did without the collaboration of her father, the intellectual Richard Lovell Edgeworth. He was born in Bath in 1744 but was destined to live out most of his life in Co. Longford, Ireland where to this day he is remembered and celebrated. He worked on his estate, continually striving to improve the conditions of his tenants. In 1787 he donated land for a Catholic chapel to be built and contributed to its construction. In the 1798 Rebellion, he defended his locality against the French, but loyalists suspected him of being a traitor, because he criticised the tyranny and ill-treatment of a corrupt government. He fled with his family to Longford town. The Catholics of his estate joined the French but at the same time they protected Edgeworth House. Later Richard was stoned by Orange supporters, after visiting the battlefield of Ballinamuck. He was stunned with the fanaticism of the Catholics and Orangemen, writing "I have lived in Ireland for no other motive than a sense of duty and a desire to improve the circle around me. I shall lose about £10,000 sunk in the country by removal, but I shall live the remainder of my life amongst men instead of warring savages". In 1799 he declined a peerage and £10.000 to vote for the Union, because of the corruption involved.

He was a great engineer; he was first in initiating a new system of road structure but it is said that the famous Macadam received the credit. His ambition was to develop the bogs in central Ireland and as one of the engineers of Arthur Wellesley's commission, devised a drainage and transportation system for bog land in Co. Longford and Co. Meath. Sadly, the vested interests of local and Absentee Landlords blocked government backing. His cutting-edge ideas of the time became a reality with the setting up of Bord na Mona 100 years later.

Relentlessly fighting in Parliament for the education of Irish children he declared in 1799 that "the power of the sword is great, but the power of education is greater". His proposals including teacher training, and a school in each parish with a playground for games, were vetoed by Parliament. In 1816 he founded in Edgeworthstown a school for boys, Catholic and Protestant, poor and rich, alike. He died later that year, his last words were 'I die with the soft feeling of gratitude to my friends and submission to God who made us' (The *Life and Letters of Maria Edgeworth*).

The Great Famine - The American people send food to 'Maria Ireland'

Maria was six when she came to Ireland, and 82 when she died at her Edgeworthstown home in May 1849. During the great Famine of 1845-1849 she and her family did their utmost to lessen the sufferings of the starving Irish. It showed how much she was loved in America when her plea for help was answered with large quantities of flour and rice shipped from Boston and addressed to 'Maria Ireland'. She stayed with her family and estate workers who barely survived. Sometime before her death she wrote these lines to Harriet. (*Chosen letters*) -

Ireland with all thy faults, thy follies too,
I love thee still: still with a candid eye must view
Thy wit, too quick, still blundering into sense
Thy reckless humour; sad improvidence,
And even what sober judges follies call,
I looking at the heart, forget them all!'

In Edgeworthstown today the memory of the generosity of the family survives as Cardinal Daly's address to the Edgeworthstown Society confirms. "Edgeworth's patriotism was qualified, his nationalism conditioned by the inevitable ambivalence of the colonist. But he still has a place in the prehistory of modern Irish nationalism, and it would be narrow-minded to exclude him from this place, a man whom the British loyalists in 1798 regarded as a renegade and suspected of treachery. The Edgeworth family, from which our town derives its name have a place in Irish annals which it would be hard to deny, and deserve a place in our affections which is understandably refused to most members of their class, the landlords of eighteenth and nineteenth century Ireland". (Dr Cahal B. Daly Bishop of Ardagh and Clonmacnois in his address to the Edgeworth Society.)

Maria's artistic achievements, her naturalistic convincing dialogue and sense of the country people and their lives were all new things in the literature of fiction which clearly inspired the Russian author Turgenev and the romantic novelist Walter Scott. But the like-minded Maria can be seen as a close literary companion to Jane Austen. They travelled life's highway at the same time. Single woman in a male dominated society, they were both courageous, prolific writers with similar values and a shared moral code to express. The established and successfully published Maria, whose passion for education made its theories an important aspect of her work, was an inspiring role model for Jane to learn from and emulate. Maria's glittering social life she could read about and perhaps hear about through family links, whilst the quality of her writing and breadth of knowledge were a guide and standard to help measure her own ideas.

CHAPTER 8

A CHORUS OF DRAMATISTS

My love for anything theatrical began in Primary school with the Christmas and summer plays. Later in Secondary school, we read Shakespeare's *Hamlet*, *As You Like It*, and *The Merchant of Venice*. Our teachers also took us to the beautiful Cork Opera House to see these plays which made me feel grown-up. The amateur dramatics of Jane's youth reminded me of a time after my mother died. Our lovely cousin Eileen would come to our house of an evening and act little plays with us girls until my dad came home from work. I remember the excitement in our front room waiting for the blanket (the screen) to be pulled back for Cinderella or some other fairy tale. Watching it all was pure magic and the pain and grief of recently losing our mother was fused with the happy feelings of these times. Eileen was handicapped, unable to walk, and her handsome husband John would call to take her home. He would always give us a riddle to solve, so ending the evening in fun and hilarity.

The late Eighteenth Century, when Jane Austen lived, was a great age of stage comedy and was one of the revival periods in British Theatre. Oliver Goldsmith and Richard Brinsley Sheridan, both Irishmen, were part of this revival. They looked back to a time when the restoration of King Charles II ushered in a new era in drama (Restoration drama 1660-1710). It had acerbity of wit, elegant language and comedy and once again two of its foremost dramatists were the Irish educated William Congreve (1670-1729) and

Londonderry born George Farquhar (1678-1707).

Amateur dramatics were a source of much fun and creativity in Jane Austen's early life and later her passion for the theatre made her the consummate theatre goer. She was attuned to the writing style of the drama which is very apparent in her novels with their long stretches of dialogue. She became a keen critic and many of her comments on the quality and variety of performance have survived in her letters. The precious years from 1811 to 1814 were probably some of the most exciting of Jane's life. By 1813 she had two of her great novels published and in November 1814 was about to have *Mansfield Park* accepted for publication. Frequently she was staying with her brother Henry in London, where the sumptuous theatres of the West End provided exciting evening entertainment. This was the icing on the cake for Jane.

In April 1811, she writes from Sloane St. Chelsea to Cassandra. "We did go to the play after all on Saturday, we went to the Lyceum and saw The Hypocrite an old play taken from Moliere's Tartuffe, and were well entertained" (Lt 70). In September 1813, now staying at Henrietta St. Covent Garden, she gives Cassandra a detailed account of her outings to the theatre. "Fanny and the two little girls are gone to take places for to-night at Covent Garden; 'Clandestine Marriage' and 'Midas'. The latter will be a fine show for L. and M. They revelled last night in 'Don Juan,' whom we left in Hell at half-past eleven. We had Scaramouche and a ghost, and were delighted. I speak of them, my delight was very tranquil, and the rest of us were sober-minded. 'Don Juan' was the last of three musical things. 'Five hours at Brighton,' in three acts - of which one was over before we arrived, none the worse - and the 'Beehive,' rather less flat and trumpery" (Lt 82). She wrote to her brother Frank again in September 1813 "Of our three evenings in town one was spent at the Lyceum and another at Covent Garden; - The Clandestine Marriage was the most respectable of the performances, the rest were sing-song and trumpery, but did very well for Lizzy and Marianne, who were indeed delighted; - but I wanted better acting.- There was no actor worthy naming - I believe the Theatres are thought at a low ebb at present" (Lt 85). With a sense of disappointment, her letter to Cassandra from Henry's home, written on the 2nd March 1814, told of "no good places to be got in Drury Lane for the next fortnight" (Lt 92). Then 3 days later, in another letter, the great actor Edmund

Kean was the subject. "We were quite satisfied with Kean. I cannot imagine better acting; but the part was too short". Later she writes, "I shall like to see Kean again excessively, & to see him with you too; - it appeared to me as if there were no fault in him anywhere" (Lt 93). When she writes to Cassandra again on the 9th March she had been to Covent Garden for two successive nights to see *The Devil to Pay* and *The Farmer's wife* 'a Musical thing in 3 Acts' with her brother Edward (Lt 94). In November 1814, she visited the theatre in London for the last time. Writing to her niece Anne, she commented on the young Irish actress Elizabeth O Neill "We were all at the play last night to see Miss O'Neal in *Isabella*. I do not think she was quite equal to my expectation. I fancy I want something more than can be. Acting seldom satisfies me. I took two pocket handkerchiefs, but had very little occasion for either. She is an elegant creature however & hugs Mr Younge delightfully" (Lt 105).

A short history of the London Theatre from the Roman times to 1800

Jane was both a theatre lover and a history lover and one imagines her knowing something of the history of the magnificent theatres of London. Like 'Rome', the theatreland of London was not 'built in a day', it took several centuries to emerge. The Roman influence with its amphitheatres gave way to tournaments, minstrels, carnivals and pageantry. The Medieval period had mystery plays based on the life of Christ as well as miracle plays based on a biblical story or the life of a saint. In the 14th century, morality plays acted out the battle between virtue and vice. After the Reformation (16th Century) came 'interludes', moral plays, at times farcical leading to a sermon at the close. In London, stages were built in the courtyards of great Inns, like the Bell in Gracechurch St. where 'spectacle' masques, music, dancing and singing were popular. The Great Halls of early Tudor nobility followed, one built around 1535 at Hampton Court Palace.

The Elizabethan Theatre (1562-1603) was considered to be the most brilliant period in the history of English Theatre. Its playhouses, built mostly outdoors, were the first permanently built theatres. In the 16th Century, the City of London chiefs would not allow theatres to be built within its square mile. Elsewhere came the rise of the professional theatre, with the licensing and censorship of plays and patronage of actors. In 1567 the Red Lion was a purpose-built

Playhouse in Mile End for touring Tudor theatrical companies. A playhouse aptly called The Theatre was built at Shoreditch where it obtained long term agreements with companies based there, a radical practice for the time. By 1572 theatre was becoming 'secular, professional, and regulated' (*The British Theatre* p 69). In 1576 The Curtain theatre was built near Shoreditch, it occasionally also supplied bear baiting. Here the poor paid one penny, a tradition other theatres adopted.

The Golden Age of Elizabethan drama evolved on the south shore of the Thames, called Bankside, with the building of The Rose in 1587 and The Swan in 1592. Here the great comedies and tragedies of Marlowe (1564-1593), Shakespeare (1564-1616), Jonson (1572-1637) and Heywood (1573-1641) were performed. Companies were developing while techniques of staging became enhanced. Shakespeare built The Globe in 1599 at Bankside where he staged his own plays with the King's Men's Company. An open-air theatre named The Fortune was built in 1600 in Finsbury, North London. I mention it because its architectural plans have survived for posterity. It had a circular open yard surrounded by three tiers of galleries and a rectangular stage covered by a canopy. It cost £520 to build at the time.

When King James I, a great theatre lover, came to the throne in 1603 he granted a licence to The Globe and Shakespeare's men became known as the King's Players. In this era (1603-1625) a tragedy was often followed by a 'jig', a playlet of song and dance with a clown supplying farce. King James had a permanent stage built in the Palace of Whitehall in 1622 for the performance of Masques. Theatres had now moved indoors, and the building of them shifted to north of the Thames.

The other side of the river Thames leading to greater theatrical glories

The hub of Theatreland was now moving to the West End of London where the first of many theatres, The Cockpit, was built in 1617. Soon Drury Lane and Covent Garden had many more wooden built theatres. In all, 15 theatres were built around London during the reign of Charles I (1625-1649), himself a keen theatregoer and favourite Stuart king of Jane Austen. Later, during the English Civil War (1642-1660), Cromwell's Puritan Parliament closed all the theatres and had Charles I beheaded. Actors were unable to work at the time but performances continued in Private houses and in taverns outside the city.

In 1660, with the restoration of the monarchy, King Charles II was brought from France. He quickly commanded the reopening of the theatres. He issued patents for two new theatres to be built and two new companies of players to be formed. The first theatre built was the glorious Theatre Royal Drury Lane which opened its doors in 1663 prospering under the king's keen support. Charles also issued a royal warrant stating that all female roles should be played by women, and his mistress, Nell Gwynn (1651-1685), became one of the first actresses of Drury Lane. In 1671, the most lavishly magnificent of all the Restoration theatres, the Dorset Garden Theatre, was built in Fleet St. For reasons unknown, it was demolished in 1709. The Queen's theatre Haymarket opened in 1707 with Irishman George Farquhar's play *The Beaux Stratagem*.

In 1714 the Hanoverian George I came to the throne and in the theatre English Pantomime was born. Men like David Garrick of Drury Lane and John Rich manager of Lincoln's Inn Fields theatre secured a place for this mixture of comic, farce and fairy-tale entertainment. Then in 1728 John Rich commissioned *The Beggar's Opera* from composer John Gay which became a stunning success. Rich built the Theatre Royal Covent Garden from its profits, and it opened in 1732 with Irish educated William Congreve's play *The Way of The World*. Ironically, *The Beggar's Opera* was not an opera in the 'Grand' mode as it used familiar tunes of the day and its characters were the ordinary people. Yet, today John Rich's theatre is known as the Royal Opera House.

From 1741 more theatres were built for London's growing population including The Lyceum near the Strand which opened in 1765. A summer patent was granted for the Little Theatre Haymarket in 1766. The Pantheon, which was built on the south side of Oxford St, opened in 1772 but was converted into an opera house in 1789. It burned down in 1792, opened its doors again in 1798. Henry Austen had a box here and it is very likely that this was the theatre Jane alluded to when she wrote to Cassandra in Sept. 1813 "I talked to Henry at the play last night. We were in a private box - Mr Spencer's - which made it much more pleasant. The box is directly on the stage.

One is infinitely less fatigued than in the common way" (Lt 82). Today, Marks and Spencers store is built on its site.

Bath, Bristol and Southampton

In the provinces, the Theatre Royal Bath was built in 1750 the most important theatre built outside London. It was rebuilt in 1805 on a different site in Beaufort Square. Jane lived in Bath from 1801 to 1806 but there is no mention of going to the theatre in her letters. In Southampton, the first theatre was built in 1766 in French Street. Bristol Theatre also built in 1766, was made a Theatre Royal in 1778 and is the oldest surviving theatre outside London. It is known today as the Bristol Old Vic.

The Irish dramatists of the Restoration which Jane delighted in.

During the Restoration, drama had reached its height in the work of William Congreve (1670-1729) who had been brought to Ireland as a child and educated at school in Kilkenny and later at Trinity College, Dublin. The Congreve family were Royalists and Congreve's father was an agent in Ireland for James Brydges who later became the 1st Duke of Chandos. He was also one of Jane's ancestors.

Jane found an affinity in Congreve's play *The Way of The World* (1700) which can be found in *Emma*.

In Congreve's play Mirabell can love Millamant, not only with her faults but even for them, "Her follies are so natural, or so artful, that they become her; and those affectations which in another woman would be odious, serve but to make her more agreeable" (1, iii). In *Emma* Mr Knightley believing that Emma is in love with Frank Churchill departs for London to stay with his brother. On hearing the news by letter that Frank has become engaged to Jane Fairfax he immediately returns to Highbury to comfort Emma, 'He had ridden home through the rain...to see how this sweetest and best of all creatures, faultless in spite of all her faults, bore the discovery' (p 433). Emma not only charms Mr Knightley but also charms her readers.

Other influential writers linked to Ireland from the Restoration era were the Irish dramatists George Farquhar (1678-1707) and Susanna Centlivre (1667-1723). Farquhar wrote *The Recruiting Officer* in 1706, followed by *The Beaux Stratagem* in 1707, two of the last grand, bawdy and cynically witty Restoration comedies. Farquhar was very ill while writing *The Beaux Stratagem* and died soon after its completion. Susanna Centlivre ran away from home and began her acting career in Dublin. She was widowed twice before she was twenty, and then started to establish her reputation as a poet and playwright. She was friendly with many of the playwrights of the time including Farquhar and contributed prologues to their plays, while they contributed to hers. Among her many successful plays was *The Gamester* produced at the Theatre Royal, Drury Lane in 1705, and ironically over 100 years later, Jane Austen had as one of the 'best plays' that might be acted by the young people in *Mansfield Park* (p 130). Centlivre was interested in politics and after Queen Anne's death predicted the coming of the Hanoverians in her poem *A Woman's Case*. She also dedicated her most famous play *The Wonder: A Woman Keeps a Secret* (1714) to George I. Decades later, in the summer of 1787, this vibrant comedy was the first to be performed by the Austens in their Steventon barn where 'all the young folk are to take part' with Jane's beautiful cousin, Eliza de Feuillide in the leading role.

The end of the Restoration period heralded a shift from bawdiness and crude language to a new style of reformed comedy. Queen Anne had an influence when she decreed in 1704 that 'all the indecency and abuses of the stage' be removed. One of the leaders of this change was Dublin man Richard Steele (1672) whose play *The Conscious Lovers* (1723) was a typical example. Its sentimental dialogue between the hero and heroine created an emotional impact which audiences came to admire and expect.

The theatrical revival inspired by Restoration theatre - And Jane Austen begins to write

In the last quarter of the 18th Century, theatregoers reacted against the 'Cult of sensibility' which had become extremely foolish in its sentimental overload. Crucial to this dramatic change, were two Irishmen, Oliver Goldsmith and Richard Brinsley Sheridan, who revived aspects of the Restoration theatre but without its cruelty and cynicism. Their humorous satire avoids these aspects, with the endings of their plays promising happiness after problems are resolved. Just like these playwrights, Jane's *Juvenilia* ridicules sentimental extravagance. Her novels are witty and satirical leading to happy endings.

In 1772 Oliver Goldsmith wrote an essay on the Theatre attacking the 'Weeping' sentimental comedy in which 'the distresses, rather that the faults of mankind make our interest in the piece'. He favoured the traditional role of comedy where foolishness is corrected by ridicule. In 1773 Goldsmith's play, *She Stoops to Conquer*, opened at the Theatre Royal Covent Garden. It is still a favourite with theatre lovers because of its consciously farcical situations encased in witty dialogue and devoid of false sentiment. Yet it has an engaging romantic couple, Constance and Hastings. Another character is Charles Marlow, who suffers from crippling shyness when expected to make fashionable conversation with a young girl of his own class, but he can rattle on boldly with 'females of another class' (1, ii). Kate Hardcastle, capable and witty, becomes a servant at an inn in a bid to captivate Charles. A theme of appearance and reality explored very much at the time. Later Jane Austen has many such themes in her novels.

Oliver Goldsmith's journey

Born in Ireland in 1728 (either at Pallas, near Ballymahon Co. Longford or at Elphin Co. Roscommon) Oliver Goldsmith survived Smallpox at an early age but his face was permanently disfigured. He attended schools at Elphin, Athlone and Edgeworthstown and with financial help from relatives he entered Trinity College, Dublin in 1744 as a Sizar. When his clergyman father died leaving little money the young Oliver had to leave Trinity in 1747. Soon his life became full of adventure as he ran away to Cork attempting to get to America but failed. Back in Ballymahon he spent some time telling stories and playing traditional Irish music on the flute. In 1752, with help from his relatives once again, he went to Edinburgh to study Medicine but failed to graduate. It was the custom of the time for the sons of the rich, on the completion of their studies, to embark on the Grand Tour of Europe. Oliver, who was penniless did go on the Grand Tour, but for him it was a walking tour and he earned his keep by busking. It is said he visited places like Padua and Paris and Switzerland. He returned to London destitute and failed to secure several positions he applied for in the Medical field. He lived around Islington and began to write. One of his sayings is 'Our greatest glory consists not in never failing, but in Rising every time we fail'. He moved near the Old Bailey, an area which housed many booksellers and publishers and one of them was a John Newbery in St. Paul's Churchyard who later published many of Oliver's works.

In 1760 Oliver wrote 98 'Chinese' letters which were later published with the title *The Citizen of the World*. One letter has the Chinese visitor classify the status of the theatregoers at the Theatre Royal, Drury Lane. In the upper gallery were the poorest who acted as if they were master of ceremonies, calling for music. Those in the boxes became part of the spectacle, "Gentlemen and ladies ogled each other through spectacles; for my companion observed that blindness was of late become fashionable, all affected indifference and ease while their hearts at the same time burned for conquest".

Then came his much-loved poem, *The Traveller*, in 1764 which was most likely based on his European adventures. He caught the spirit of the age with these lines - Where wealth and freedom reign, contentment fails, and honour sinks where commerce long prevails. The Industrial Revolution was well under way in England and beginning on the Continent. But it was a more peaceful time before the American and French Revolutions changed the world for ever.

Goldsmith's best loved novel, *The Vicar of Wakefield*, was published in 1766 and is still considered one of the masterpieces of the English language. It was by chance that his friend Samuel Johnson called one morning to visit a distressed Oliver who had been arrested by his landlady for non-payment of rent. Johnson saw the Manuscript on a table ready for the Press, took it to a publisher and Goldsmith received 60 guineas for it. He lived the remainder of his life in London. It is said that he was a little vain and sensitive, but his charity and kindliness were legendary. He was greatly loved in his later years. He died in April 1774 at the age of forty-six and was buried in the Temple, in the City of London. A monument was erected to his memory in Westminster Abbey, with an epitaph by Johnson and a statue of him was built in Ballymahon, Co. Longford, Ireland.

Jane Austen and Oliver Goldsmith

Jane Austen read and admired the writings of Oliver Goldsmith from a very young age. She read *The Traveller* and his *History of England* and it is likely that she got the idea for her own comic *History'* from his work. She also read *The Vicar of Wakefield*. In *Emma*, Harriet Smith tells Emma that Mr Martin, a respected farmer "has read *The Vicar of Wakefield*' (*E* p 29). Mr Martin's character is seen to be reflected in his choice of reading material, and is also endorsed by Mr Knightley, who stresses to Emma that Mr Martin will make Harriet a good husband.

Also in *Emma*, when Frank Churchill's aunt dies, Jane Austen in her narrative pays direct tribute to Goldsmith's poem from *The Vicar of Wakefield*. 'A sudden seizure…had carried her off…The great Mrs Churchill was no more…Everybody had a degree of gravity and sorrow; tenderness towards the departed, solicitude for the surviving friends…curiosity to know where she would be buried. Goldsmith tells us, that when lovely woman stoops to folly, she has nothing to do but to die; and when she stoops to be disagreeable, it is equally to be recommended as a clearer of ill-fame. Mrs Churchill, after being disliked at least twenty-five years, was now spoken of with compassionate allowances' (*E* p 387).

"When lovely woman stoops to folly;
And finds too late that men betray
What charm can soothe her melancholy,
What art can wash her guilt away?
The only art her guilt to cover,
To hide her shame from every eye,
To give repentance to her lover,
And wring his bosom - is to die."

Jane has Goldsmith's lovingly nostalgic poem on rural life *The Deserted Village* (1770) in mind when Emma takes Frank Churchill on a walk around Highbury. As they 'pause…at the Crown Inn' she tells him that it has a large room "built many years ago for a ball-room" but the young people moved to the town and "such brilliant days had long passed away" (*E* p 197). Below is part of Goldsmith's poem.

Sweet Auburn! loveliest village of the plain;
Where health and plenty cheered the labouring swain,
Where smiling spring its earliest visit paid,
And parting summer's lingering blooms delayed…..
And trembling shrinking from the spoiler's hand
Far, far away thy children leave the land

Ill fares the land, to hastening ills a prey,
Where wealth accumulates, and men decay.

Jane's imagination absorbed the ideas of Irish playwrights Arthur Murphy and Hugh Kelly

The prodigious Arthur Murphy was born in 1727 in Co. Roscommon and made his first appearance as Shakespeare's *Othello* at the Theatre Royal Covent Garden in 1754. He then turned his talents to playwriting. One of his popular plays was *The Way to Keep Him* (1760), a comedy involving themes of women who stop bothering to please their husbands, and the louche behaviour of men in fashionable society. In 1787 so many parliamentarians were attending its performance at Richmond House that a proposal had to be deferred in the House of Commons (P. Byrne p 1). In 1807 Jane Austen took her niece, Fanny, to the theatre in French St. Southampton to see *The Way to Keep Him*. One of its characters is ashamed of being in love with his wife and calls her his 'Cara Sposa'. In *Emma*, the ill-bred Mrs Elton hails her husband "my Caro Sposo" which prompts Emma to call her "A little upstart, vulgar being, with her Mr E and her Caro Sposo" (*E* pp 278/279).

Hugh Kelly, born in Killarney in 1739, had his comedy, *False Delicacy* produced by Garrick at the Theatre Royal Drury Lane in 1768. This concept of *False Delicacy* is found in Jane Austen's *Mansfield Park* where it appears confirmed by "True Delicacy". Mrs Norris praises Maria for her "strict sense of propriety, so much of that true delicacy which one seldom meets with nowadays" (*MP* p 117). When the young Bertrams decide to stage *Lovers Vows* against the wishes of their absent father, Edmund pleads with Maria to stop the theatricals "You must set the example. If others have blundered, it is your place to put them right, and show them what true delicacy is" (*MP* p 140). But Maria's delicacy is false, she ignores her brother's pleas and her father's wishes. In contrast her cousin Fanny, niece of Sir Thomas exemplifies true delicacy in refusing to enter into the theatricals. As Edmund says to his father on his return "Fanny is the only one who has judged rightly throughout" (*MP* p 187). Later when Fanny refuses to marry the rich, but unprincipled, Henry Crawford, Sir Thomas calls her 'wilful and perverse' though he knows in his heart that she is 'very timid, and... nervous' (*MP* p 320). He sends her away, but Fanny who has 'true delicacy' is eventually shown to have made the right decision.

Theatre-land was enhanced with actors and actresses from the Emerald Isle - enter the 'Rant'

The input of elegance and expressive form of the Gaelic language seems to have energised the language and literature of the significant Anglo-Irish writers of Jane Austen's time. Apart from the management and investment in practical stagecraft which Sheridan offered in addition to his writing, a large contingent of successful Irish actors, male and female added vibrancy to the London theatres. It is possible to speculate that Jane appreciated their artistic contributions even if unaware of their origin.

Charles Macklin (1699-1797) was born in Co. Donegal, and acted in the Theatre Royal, Dublin when Richard Sheridan's father Thomas was the manager. In London, his greatest role was Shylock in *The Merchant of Venice* which he performed in the 1740s. Theatre lore tells us of him being so 'chilling' in the role that George II suggested bringing him into the House of Commons to subdue troublesome MPs. His last performance of Shylock was at the age of 89 but it is said that his ghost haunts the front stalls of Drury Lane to this day. There is also a street near Drury Lane named after him. Macklin wrote two popular comedies *Love a la Mode* and *Man of the World* and was the first actor to challenge the traditional method of acting and impress with his individual interpretation of role. In his portrayal of *Hamlet* his first meeting with the ghost was played with understated simplicity rather than the expected exaggerated 'starts' and 'rants'.

The rant, a style of acting for tragedy, was under attack by theatrical critics and David Garrick followed Macklin in removing such slavish devotion to this tradition. Jane Austen shows her awareness of ranting in *Mansfield Park* when she depicts amateur actor John Yates as one who 'rants' and 'starts' in the old style: 'Mr Yates was in general thought to rant dreadfully' (*MP* p 164). On the other hand, Yates dislikes Henry Crawford's 'tameness and insipidity' (*MP* p 165), while Fanny finds Henry's style 'truly dramatic' (*MP* p 337).

The legendary David Garrick, (1717-1779) who successfully presided over the Theatre Royal Drury Lane for nearly 30 years, established the style of theatre to which Jane Austen was to become familiar. The early reputation of his company was largely based on the popularity of the Irish actresses he promoted on the London stage and one of the most celebrated of this early period was Peg Woffington (1720-1760) who at the age of 17 had been the most popular performer in Dublin. She left for London at the age of 20 and made her Covent Garden debut in George Farquhar's *The Recruiting Officer*, where 'her vivacious spirit and great beauty' amazed audiences. It was said that she was the most beautiful woman who ever appeared on stage. She lived with David Garrick for many years, but her fierce temper eventually parted them. Another of his leading ladies was Dubliner Anne Bellamy (1733-1788) who made her first appearance at the Theatre Royal, Covent Garden, in 1744. She published her *Apology*, a six-volume account of her tempestuous career in the theatre which Jane would have likely read at The Rectory in Steventon

The great comedy actress Dorothy Jordan (Waterford 1762-1816) made her debut in Dublin in 1777, but fled to Leeds after her theatre manager made her pregnant in 1782. By 1785 she had moved to London, became a great success at the Theatre Royal, Drury Lane, where she remained for the next 25 years. She played Lady Teazle in Sheridan's *School for Scandal*. In 1790 she met the Duke of Clarence (later William IV) and had ten children by him. Jane Austen saw Dorothy Jordan perform her most famous part, Nell in *The Devil to Pay* at Covent Garden in 1814 (Lt 93) where Jordan delighted audiences with her transformation from a woman of low birth to an aristocrat.

The Irish actress Elizabeth O'Neill (1791-1872) had an enormous success in the role of Shakespeare's Juliet in October 1814 at the age of twenty-two. It is reported that Byron refused to see her act for fear of becoming an O'Neill convert. In November Jane Austen went to see her in *Isabella* at Covent Garden (Lt 105) the last recorded outing of Jane's to a London theatre.

Garrick encouraged the Irish actor Spranger Barry (Dublin, 1719-1777) to come to London with the promise of work in his Drury Lane productions. This was to Garrick's own cost when Barry's performance of Romeo in *Romeo and Juliet* was said to outshine his own. Barry, reputed to be very handsome, was then driven by Garrick's jealousy to work at the rival Covent Garden and their competing performances made for intense critical debate. Barry then became a builder of theatres eventually returning to Ireland where he was made manager of the newly opened Theatre Royal in Cork City in 1761.

The fabulous contribution of Michael Kelly - friend of Mozart - and Jane played their music too

Of all the Irish performers from this time the most outstanding was Michael Kelly, (1762-1826) a singer, actor, composer and later theatre manager whose reputation was established early in Italy and Vienna. The march from his famous stage work *Bluebeard* (Theatre Royal, Drury Lane,1798) is included in *Jane Austen's Music* (p 14) and is copied out by Jane herself. Michael, a decent well-bred man knew all the greats of the Drury Lane theatre of this era. His life span ran parallel to Jane Austen's and through his vivid 'Reminiscences' we get a glimpse of the other side of the footlights of that sparkling era of Sheridan and Edmund Kean and Michael himself. His voice can be heard in the mind's eye as we read in brilliant detail his descriptions of staging operas. He wrote that 'the best interests of Drury Lane were nearest his heart' (*Reminiscences* p 241).

Born in Dublin where his father was Master of Ceremonies at Dublin Castle, Michael Kelly was fortunate in getting tuition from many great Italian singers who came to stay at his father's house and piano lessons from Thomas Arne's son Michael Arne. He began his career, singing and acting in the Smock Alley theatre. Famed for his tenor voice he travelled to the Kingdom of Naples in 1779, where as a protégé of Sir William Hamilton he sang for the King and Queen. His daily tuition from Giuseppe Aprile eventually enabled him to sing in any theatre in Europe. At Livorno, he met the composer Stephen Storace and his sister Nancy aged 15 who was Prima Donna of the comic opera there. In 1784 he sang with Nancy Storace in Paisiello's *The Barber of Seville*. In Florence, Pisa and Venice he met the leading lights of Italian opera, and sang with the famous Teresa de Petris. With an Italian company, coached by the famous composer Gluck, he sang at the court of Emperor Joseph II in Vienna. Kelly became great friends with Mozart (1756-1791), singing the role of Don Curzio in his latest opera *The Marriage of Figaro*. An interesting tale has it that Michael and Mozart had a tete-a-tete regarding the duet Crudel, perche finora (They are over, Act III) disagreeing as how it should be sung. Michael won the day, and Mozart was well satisfied with the result. Nancy Storace sang the female lead.

With a wealth of knowledge and experience Michael, aged only 25, came to the Theatre Royal, Drury lane in 1787 and formed a close alliance with its successful manager another Irishman Richard Sheridan and 'had the happiness to enjoy his confidence and society' (*Reminiscences*). His Drury Lane debut was in Dibdin's *Lionel and Clarissa*, and he was coached by Thomas Linley, Sheridan's father-in-law. From 1787 he was the principal English tenor at Drury Lane. In May of that year he sang at the composer Handel's commemoration at Westminster Abbey. In 1788 he sang in Liverpool, Chester, Manchester, Worcester and Birmingham with England's greatest female singers, Mrs Crouch, Madame Mara and Nancy Storace. He knew and worked with Mrs Jordan and Mrs Siddons. In April 1789, at Drury Lane, he sang Stephen Storace's *The Haunted Tower* and it is said 'delivered a ringing top Bb'. In early 1791 more success came in another Storace opera *The Siege of Belgrade*. On the 4th June 1791, he performed in *The Country Girl* and *No Song no Supper* on the very last night of the Old Drury Lane theatre which was then demolished.

Michael went to Paris in 1793 'looking out for material for Drury Lane'. On the 24th January, he watched as King Louis XVI and Queen Antoinette were taken to the Thuillieries as prisoners. In 1793 he became acting manager of the King's theatre, Haymarket (now Her Majesty's Theatre). In 1804 he wrote the music for the first production of the pantomime Cinderella at the new Drury Lane theatre. In 1808 he went to Dublin where he sang opera with the famous Madame Catalani for six nights and they proceeded to Cork where they sang for another 6 nights. He commented on the Cork audience's passion for music (*Rem* P 242). In February 1809 as he was dining with Sheridan and others in a nearby cafe a young woman rushed in to tell them that Drury Lane theatre was in flames. They watched the inferno and he later wrote 'All the scores of the operas which I had composed for the theatre, the labour of years, were then consuming and with a heavy heart I walked home to Pall Mall' (*Reminiscences*. p 254-55). Michael made his last appearance on stage in 1811. It was in his native Dublin 'where I had made my first appearance when a boy in 1779' (*Reminiscences*). He retired that year and in 1812 he was present when 'the New Drury Lane Theatre opened with Shakespeare's *Hamlet*'.

Michael also had a connection with one of Jane Austen's favourite actors, the phenomenal Edmund Kean. On January 26th 1814 Edmund Kean (1789-1833) made his Drury Lane debut as Shylock in *The Merchant of Venice*. Michael sat in his Drury Lane seat and next to him sat Lord Byron. They were watching Edmund Kean play *Othello*, when Byron said to him, "Mr Kelly, depend upon it, this is a man of genius" (*Reminiscences* p 284). Michael was delighted that he had played a part in Kean's young life. When Kean was four years old he made his first appearance on stage as Cupid in the ballet Cymon, selected from around twenty children by Michael. Jane went to see Kean in March 1814 and wrote to Cassandra that she would like to see him again "excessively" and "there were no fault in him anywhere" (Lt 93). During his retirement, Michael wrote his 'Reminiscences' of his 25 years at the Theatre Royal Drury Lane and the King's Theatre. A kind of Arabian Nights tale of the richness of life at Drury Lane. It seems he even scandalously shared a mistress with the Prince of Wales. His grave lies at St. Paul's Church, known as the Actors' Church, Covent Garden.

Ireland's contribution to The British Theatre

From the Restoration onwards, the London stage hosted many Irish actors and actresses whose performances were amongst the most celebrated and successful. Also, the dramatic literature with which Jane was familiar with, and enjoyed, owed much to Irish input because so many celebrated dramatists were Irish, or of Irish extraction. The actors and dramatists of the time owed much of their art to an exposure of Irish phrasing and word play.

Ireland had contributed greatly to The British Theatre. The Irish academic practice of rigorous scholarship and classical training in literature laid the foundations fostering the talent of the Irish playwrights. There was the distinct advantage of the spoken literary tradition of Ireland, where from the earliest times bards and wandering storyteller musicians were held in high esteem. Irish writers often had a considerable ear for dialogue, a vital aid to playwriting. This gift of eloquence, of tales told with liveliness, wit and humour, enhanced the reputation acquired by talented Irish performers as they delivered their lines.

CHAPTER 9

SHERIDAN

One Sunday evening I went to look at the Drury Lane Theatre in London's West End. I wanted to know something of Sheridan's Drury Lane. While staring at the beautiful building a man came up and spoke to me. He was from Tuscany and owned a nearby restaurant to which he invited me for a drink. I accepted his invitation and was very glad as in minutes I was in a fascinating place which was a wonderful replica of a theatre. I had a refreshing soda water while he told me of his love for Drury Lane. This was a happy little interlude on my quest to know more about Sheridan and the great Drury Lane.

The day came when I did visit Drury Lane with a very good friend of mine. There was a tour of the theatre at three o'clock and we were the only participants. We did not get to step on the famous stage but we had a glorious tour beginning with the Green room, then walking through a corridor with its walls a visual feast of the theatre's past, great managers like Garrick, playwrights and actors, some been Irish. Our guide filled our senses with dramatic tales and anecdotes of their lives. Of course Sheridan's theatre had long been burnt down and rebuilt but our guide showed us a grill with a wall behind it and told us that it was all that remained of his theatre. He told me to put my hand through the grill and take a little pebble as a memento and I have that pebble on my mantelpiece at home. In the foyer my friend bought me a large colourful History of Drury Lane, full of paintings, pictures and particulars of its history with its fair share of shocks and surprises. The Glamour of Drury Lane remained in my thoughts for many weeks.

Lee Hunt, editor of *The Examiner*, marked the death of Richard Brinsley Sheridan on 7th July 1816 with an obituary recalling that; "he was a man of wit, a lively and elegant dramatist, a winning and powerful orator, a sound politician, a lover of real freedom, a careless liver, an Irishman in short." Sheridan's funeral was a celebration attended by dukes, earls, lords and viscounts and many men of prominence including the Lord Mayor of London who came to pay him homage before he was laid to rest in Poets Corner, Westminster Abbey. The leading romantic poet of the era Lord Byron wrote; "He has written the best comedy (*School for Scandal*), the best drama (*The Duenna*), the best farce (*The Critic*), and the best address (Monologue on Garrick); and, to crown all delivered the very best oration (the famous Begum Speech) ever…heard in this country".

In her Chawton home in Hampshire, Jane Austen would have also grieved for the passing of the Master Craftsman who had captured her imagination from a very young age. His literary accomplishment inspired Jane in all her writing from her *Juvenilia* to her unfinished novel, *Sanditon*. In 1784 when James, her elder brother, staged Sheridan's first play, *The Rivals*, while home from Oxford it made an enduring imprint on her mind. In short, Jane had come under Sheridan's spell and it lasted a lifetime. Her six great novels show structures of plot similar to *The Rivals*. Also, the theme of 'Gossip', which is what Sheridan's *The School for Scandal* is all about, can be seen to be brilliantly interwoven by Jane into all her novels.

There are several instances in Jane's writing and life which convey her ardour for Sheridan's plays. In 1791 (aged fifteen) she refers to his play *The Critic* in her *History of England*. In 1809, we read of her acting the comic role of Mrs Candour from *The School for Scandal* at her friend Mrs Heathcote's Twelfth Night Party. (Manydown, Sir William Heathcote). In 1814 Jane briefly alludes to *The Rivals* and *The School for Scandal* in her novel *Mansfield Park* (p 131).

His ancestors were the Gaelic speaking O Sioradains of County Cavan. One relative, William Sheridan made Bishop of Kilmore and Ardagh in 1681, was noted for having said that the Bible was 'almost a necessary evil…though the Word spoken be more efficacious…the

Word written is more durable'. Sheridan's grandfather, Rev. Thomas Sheridan, a schoolmaster and close friend of Dean Swift, wrote *The Art of Punning*. Sheridan's father, Thomas (1719-1788), was an actor and for a time, theatre manager of Dublin's Smock Alley and the Haymarket, London. In his book, *Rhetorical Grammar of the English Language* (1781), he declared, "Spoken language is the Gift of God, written the invention of men". Literary talent also flowed from Sheridan's mother who wrote *Memoirs of Miss Sidney Biddulph* (1761).

He tasted success at the glorious Drury Lane before the age of thirty

Born in Dublin, Ireland in 1751 Richard Brinsley Sheridan was educated at home for some years with his two sisters Lizzy and Betsy. Later he attended Harrow public school and while there his mother died. In 1770 the Sheridans moved to Bath where they became friends with Thomas Linley and his family of musicians and singers. Richard met the beautiful 16-year-old Elizabeth Linley who was gifted with a soprano voice that made her a public idol. Many men fell in love with her including Sheridan. The romance of Richard and Elizabeth displayed all the intrigue and glamour which characterised the rest of Sheridan's career in British social and political life. It began when Elizabeth told Richard's sisters that she intended to leave Bath to escape the unwelcome attentions of a Captain Thomas Matthews. They alerted Richard, who ran away to France with her. Their elopement and subsequent marriage in 1773 at Marylebone Church, London involved him in several life-threatening duels in London and Bath, with Matthews. These duels of honour which Sheridan fought to ensure his prestige as a gentleman gave him an early notoriety. It was matched by his gifted literary success in the theatre from where, multi-talented and charismatic, he was able to launch a political career. Great success came to Elizabeth when she sang for George III and his family at Buckingham Palace. Richard and Elizabeth made London their home, and in January 1775 his first play *The Rivals* opened at the Theatre Royal, Covent Garden, and in November of that year their only child Thomas was born.

Sheridan's literary career was a triumph, achieved during his twenties. In May 1777, *The School for Scandal*, said to be the English Masterpiece of comedy of manners, opened at Drury Lane. Its manager, David Garrick wrote the prologue asking "Is our young bard so young to think that he can stop the full spring tide of calumny?...So strong, so swift, the monster there's no gagging". In October 1779 Sheridan's last original work, *The Critic* (or *A Tragedy Rehearsed*), was performed there to a rapturous audience. In 1776 at the age of twenty-five Sheridan became manager of Drury Lane Theatre by buying half of the patent for £35,000 from Garrick, who "was proud of the new manager and in a triumphant manner boasted of the genius to whom he had consigned the conduct of the theatre" (Murphy, *Life of Garrick*). In the 1780s Sheridan made his father manager. These were happy years for Elizabeth and Richard and their families. Drury Lane was demolished in 1792, and after Sheridan raised £150,000 to rebuild it, he opened it with a successful benefit The Glorious 1st of June in 1794. Disaster struck in 1809 when the theatre was destroyed by fire, and it is said that as Sheridan watched the inferno raging from the Piazza Coffee House nearby he remarked, "a man may surely take a glass of wine by his own fireside".

Careering towards Westminster

In 1780 he entered Parliament and became an *MP* for Stafford. The Sheridans became one of the most celebrated couples in England, mixing in the wealthiest of circles and experiencing the glittering lifestyle of the aristocratic Devonshire House and Carlton House families. As a member of the Literary Club and Brooks's exclusive Whig club he met eminent politicians like Edmund Burke and Charles Fox, whose close friendships became important in both his public and private life. Sheridan, though lacking both finance and privilege, strove to remain free of any financial corruption and abuse of patronage. In such a stratified society, his political rivals with their aristocratic values scorned his theatrical, and worse his Irish roots. Particularly dear to his heart, was the ending of exploitation and misrule of Ireland reminding his audience that "the tyranny practised upon the Irish has been throughout unremitting". He entertained, and served well the party hierarchy, but he refused to compromise on his core beliefs, which left him isolated and eventually ineffectual, politically. Sheridan was an advocate of human rights including the education of women. He declined a title and the rewards of high office, partly to avoid compromising his independence. Much of his reputation has rested since on his theatrical achievement. Yet it was said that the masterpieces of his oratory were heard at the Great Hall

Westminster when in 1787 and 1788 he condemned Warren Hastings' corruption in India. Incidentally Jane's first cousin Eliza de Feuillide was present at the Great Hall and heard some of Sheridan's masterpieces.

Happy youth - Jane in a loving family at home in Steventon, Hampshire

Jane was born in 1775, the same year *The Rivals* was produced at Covent Garden, into a scholarly family of two girls and six boys. Their father was the Reverend George Austen, an Oxford scholar who had a library of '500 books' at their Steventon home in the heart of the Hampshire countryside. Their mother cultivated a love of rhymes, verse and word games and the children were encouraged to read aloud books and plays which became central to the family's evening entertainment. An uncle of Jane's mother, the celebrated Dr Theophilus Leigh had held the Mastership of Balliol College, Oxford, and 'was a man more famous for his sayings than his doings, overflowing with puns and witticisms and sharp retorts'. The family enjoyed amateur theatricals, usually staged in the barn at Steventon by Jane's brothers when home from their studies at Oxford. Watching from 'the wings', the stage became part of Jane's childhood play. Then during her short time at school, Mrs La Tournelle a teacher, told stories of the 'green room' at Drury Lane and so Jane's lifelong attachment to the theatre was formed.

Sheridan's influence on Jane's *Juvenilia*

When Jane began to write in her teens she sought to emulate Sheridan's sparkling wit, biting satire, and brilliant dialogue in what has come to be known as her *Juvenilia*, her childhood and teenage writings. Absurd and comical, it deliciously parodies Sheridan's plays while revealing facets of Jane's personality and great talent at a very young age. She dedicates these little plays and stories to her cherished family including Cassandra and her brothers. Above all in her *Juvenilia*, the influence of Sheridan's great comedies, *The School for Scandal* and *The Critic*, are evident.

School for Scandal is set in London's West End, where all the scandal mongers and gossips in the 'school' live. They have tag names to fit their repulsive characters; Lady Sneerwell, Snake, Mr Crabtree, his nephew Sir Benjamin Backbite, and Joseph Surface who masks his corrupt nature with a coating of bogus sentiment. Another character, Mrs Candour, is perhaps the deadliest of the scandalmongers because though she only ever tells the truth she uses it to create the maximum damage to her victims. There is Maria who makes a stand for decency throughout the play, and makes a hasty exit from the scandal mongers in the first 'Act' whispering "Their malice is intolerable" (I, i). Charles Surface, Joseph's brother though not a member of the 'School' is considered degenerate, as he drinks, overspends, and seems to lack purpose, yet he professes to have a 'good heart' and is honest. He is in love with Maria, and in the finale he "intends to set about" (V, iii) reforming as he is soon to marry her. In the play, Sheridan attacks hypocrisy, malice and false feelings with language full of sharp witty dialogue.

The School for Scandal and Jane's *Jack and Alice*

Jane, in her early teens, wrote a short comedy *Jack and Alice* (*MW* pp 12/29) and it is obvious that one of her characters, Lady Williams, is a take-off of Mrs Candour. Jane pushes romantic humour to farcical extremes when Alice Johnson, who is in love with the insufferable Charles Adams, visits Lady Williams after drinking too much wine "to seek a relief for her disordered Head & Love-sick Heart" (*MW* p 15). Lady Williams who uses her "candour" to the disadvantage of others tells Alice the story of her life and describes Mrs Watkins a relative as "esteemed a pretty Woman, but I never thought her very handsome...

She had too high a forehead, Her eyes were too small & she had too much colour".

Alice angrily interrupts "Do you think that anyone can have too much colour?"

"Indeed I do...when a person has too great a degree of red in their Complexion it gives their face in my opinion, too red a look"

"But Madam I deny that it is possible for anyone to have too great a proportion of red in their Cheeks".

As they argue, Alice's father, Mr Johnson, arrives and "with some difficulty forced her away from Lady Williams, Mrs Watkins & her red cheeks" (*MW* pp 17/18). This scene of Jane's directly echoes the following scene from *The School for Scandal*, where huge exaggeration is a vibrant part of the humour, as Mrs Candour shows her hypocrisy-

> Mrs Candour. They'll not allow our friend Miss Vermillion to be handsome.
> Lady Sneerwell. Oh, surely she is a pretty woman.
> Crabtree. I am very glad you think so, ma'am.
> Mrs Candour. She has a charming fresh colour.
> Lady Teazle. Yes, when it is fresh put on.
> Mrs Candour. ...I'll swear her colour is natural. I have seen it come and go.
> Lady Teazle. I dare swear you have, ma'am: it goes off at night, and comes again in the morning (II, ii).

Lady Williams, again like Mrs Candour, has a voracious craving for gossip and herself and Alice on meeting, "'A lovely young woman apparently in great pain' asks her to "favour us with your Life & adventures?". Later Lady Williams gossips to this young woman about Alice saying "She has many rare & charming qualities, but Sobriety is not one of them. The whole Family are…a sad drunken set…more particularly Alice…She is indeed a most pleasing Girl! I shall always love her!" (*MW* p 23). Lady Williams can be summed up as Maria summed up Mrs Candour in *The School for Scandal*, "with a very gross affectation of good nature and benevolence, she does more mischief than the direct malice of old Crabtree" (1, i).

Lucy 'fell a sacrifice to the Envy & Malice of Sukey' (*MW* p 28)

Jane, even at the age of twelve, shows a great understanding of Sheridan's characters. In *Jack and Alice*, she creates her own Sukey Simpson in the mould of Sheridan's Lady Sneerwell. But where Lady Sneerwell takes pleasure in killing her characters metaphorically and, 'can do more with a word or look than many can with the most laboured detail' (*School for Scandal* 1, i) Jane has the 'envious and malevolent' Sukey Simpson really kill the 'amiable & lovely' Lucy who was about to marry a rich elderly Duke. Sukey, jealous of Lucy's superior charms 'took her by poison from an admiring World at the age of seventeen' (*MW* p 28).

"They have mangled my play in a most shocking manner"

(Puff - *The Critic*, III)

Jane shared with Sheridan a love of the ridiculous and was susceptible to his marvellous burlesque *The Critic*, imitating its nonsensical situations in *Love and Friendship*, *Lesley Castle*, and her comic *History of England*. She wrote them all in her teens.

The Critic itself revolves around the production and performance of a play and much of the humour is derived from the antics of all those involved in the process. It was said that Sheridan suffered from critics and dabblers so much that he used his incredible gift for mockery and hit back at them all with *The Critic*. Once again, the characters all have tag names such as Sneer, the spiteful and sarcastic critic, Sir Fretful Plagiary the playwright, who loves flattery, hates criticism, and thinks his plays are perfect. There is the affected Mr Dangle who likes showing off while his wife makes sharp gibes at his expense. Finally comes Mr Puff skilled in the theory and practise of 'puffing' and mock publicity. His gigantic personality and pompous language dominates the play, while his vanity and incompetence as a playwright makes *A Tragedy Rehearsed* into a shambles. He attempts to imitate Shakespeare with his fake heroic speeches and 'flowery' language. Sheridan's sense of the ridiculous in *The Critic* inspired Jane to create her over the top caricatures in the hilarious *Love and Friendship* (*MW* pp 76/109) where she shows her delight in theatrical clout and gesture.

In the theatre of the time the cult of sensibility was reflected in the "faint", the privilege of a delicate heroine. Sheridan enjoyed using such a tactic for dramatic outcome, irony, and laughter in *The Critic* where the recently reunited relatives "faint alternately in each other's arms" (III). Jane exploits this tactic with greater exaggeration in *Love and Friendship* where there is much talk of fainting with even an alternative faint onto a sofa at one point. Later one of the characters, Laura, writes about an "unexpected Blow to our Gentle Sensibility…we could only faint" (*MW* p 89) and is warned "Beware of swoons…Run mad as often as you chuse; but do not faint-" (*MW* p 102).

His 'mad' scene in *The Critic* and her 'mad' scene in *Love and Friendship*

Sheridan's mad scene for Tilburina in *The Critic*, is in an inflated and histrionic style, (said to be a caricature of Ophelia's madness in *Hamlet*, IV).

> *The wind whistles - the moon rises - see,*
> *They have killed my squirrel in his cage!*
> *Is this a grasshopper? - Ha! No; it is my*
> *Whiskerandos - you shall not keep him -*
> *I know you have him in your pocket -*
> *An oyster may be crossed in love! - Who says*
> *A whale's a bird? - Ha! did you call, my love? -*
> *He's here! he's there! - He's everywhere!*
> *Ah me! He's nowhere!*
>   (The Critic III)

In *Love and Friendship*, Jane goes further and constructs her mad scene in an even more bizarre way than Sheridan. After Laura and Sophia find their husbands 'weltering in their blood', Laura describes her own madness -

'My Eyes assumed a vacant stare, my face became as pale as Death, and my Senses were considerably impaired - "Talk not to me of Phaetons (said I, raving in a frantic, incoherent manner) - Give me a violin -, I'll play to him and sooth him...Beware ye gentle Nymphs of Cupid's Thunderbolts, avoid the piercing Shafts of Jupiter - Look at that Grove of Firs - I see a Leg of Mutton - They told me Edward was not Dead; but they deceived me - they took him for a Cucumber" Thus I continued wildly exclaiming on my Edward's Death - For two Hours did I rave thus madly' (*MW* p 100).

In *The Critic*, Sheridan pokes fun at the pomposity of the 'history plays' popular at the time. Jane too, at the age of fifteen, adopts an irreverent and humorous approach in her 'partial and prejudiced' *History of England* and Sheridan and *The Critic* are singled out. She declares, 'Sir Walter Raleigh flourished in this and the preceding reign, and is by many people held in great veneration and respect - But as he was an enemy of the noble Essex, I have nothing to say in praise of him, and...refer...to Mr Sheridan's play of *The Critic*, where they will find...interesting anecdotes as well of him as of his friend Sir Christopher Hatton' (*MW* p 148).

One 'interesting anecdote' Jane refers to appears in Puff's rehearsal of *The Spanish Armada* (II, ii) when Sir Walter Raleigh meets

Sir Christopher Hatton. Puff declares to those watching the rehearsal "You'll know Sir Christopher by his turning out his toes - famous...for his dancing. I like to preserve all the little traits of character" (II, ii). Hatton's language turns a serious situation into a farce.

> *Hatton...And valour-breathing trumpet's shrill appeal,*
> *Responsive vibrate on my listening ear...*
> *Raleigh...O most accomplished Christopher! - I find*
> *Thy staunch sagacity still tracks the future,*
> *In the fresh print of the overtaken past...*
> *(II, ii)*

In real life, in the year 1584, the Lord Chancellor, Sir Christopher Hatton, is recorded to have led 400 kneeling members of Parliament in a prayer for Queen Elizabeth's safety. Once again Sheridan, in a nod towards this event, in *The Spanish Armada*, has the characters of Sir Walter Raleigh and Sir Christopher Hatton kneel in prayer on stage while Puff asks them, "You could not go off kneeling, could you?" (II, ii).

The Critic and 'Lackeys of literature' - *Lesley Castle* and "Bravo, Bravissimo"

Sheridan, later in life, voiced his opinion that Act 1 of *The Critic* was his best work. It opens with Mrs Dangle expressing annoyance with Mr Dangle's obsession with the theatre as she scolds him, "Why can't you ride your hobby horse without desiring to place me on a pillion behind you, Mr Dangle?" and grumbles to Sneer of the "lackeys of literature" and the "Signors and Signoras" her husband brings home. Sneer adds to her list with "solicited solicitations" and "follies and foibles" (I,i). It is evident that Jane was also clearly delighted with Act 1 of *The Critic* and adopts similar alliterative patterning. in *Lesley Castle*, "my sister came running to me...her face as White as a Whipt syllabub" (*MW* p 113) and "as cool as a cream-cheese" (*MW* p 130). Sheridan has Mr Dangle praising the Italian singers with "Bravo!...bravissimo! Admirablissimo! (I, ii) and once again Jane outdoes him in *Lesley Castle* having Charlotte 'hollow' at Eloisa's playing, "Bravo, Bravissimo, Encore, Da capo, allegretto, con expressione, and Poco presto with many other such outlandish words...expressive of my admiration" (*MW* p 130).

Before 1800, while living in Steventon, Jane wrote drafts of her first three novels; *Sense and Sensibility*, *Pride and Prejudice*, and *Northanger Abbey*. In 1801, her father retired and the family went to live in Bath. Her father died in 1805, and the family returned to Hampshire in 1809. They took up residence at Chawton village, in a house gifted to them by Jane's brother, Edward. He had been adopted by the Knights, an aristocratic family from Kent when he was ten years old and had inherited land in Hampshire which included the house that Jane and her family came to live in. It was at Chawton that she wrote the three novels of her maturity; *Mansfield Park*, *Emma*, and *Persuasion*.

From her first novel onwards Jane's affinity to the theatre is entrenched

Long stretches of dialogue and frequent use of theatrical terms are part of her novels. In *Pride and Prejudice* Darcy fears "that the performance would reflect no credit on either" (p 94). Emma says to Harriet "It is a sort of prologue to the play...and will be soon followed by matter-of-fact prose" (*E* p 74) and Jane Fairfax tells Emma "I had always a part to act" (*E* p 459). Anne Elliot is aware of Mrs Clay's 'good acting' in *Persuasion* (p 213).

"Jack, such eyes!...Not a glance but speaks and kindles some thought of love!"

In the theatre of the time, exaggerated eye direction, movement and contact was a heavily used mechanism to emphasise character, intent and emotional state. The great actor and manager of Drury Lane, David Garrick elicited excited comments from Hannah More on his "most eloquent expression of the eye" in *Hamlet*, and the poet Charles Churchill remarked on his "strange powers which lie within the magic circle of the Eye". This stress on "the look" or stare, was employed and developed by the great popular actors and actresses of the era, Kemble, Siddons and later, Edmund Kean.

Sheridan also highlights the expressive potential of the eye for dramatic effect.

In *The Rivals*, Sir Anthony makes his son Jack aware of Lydia's beautiful eyes:

"Jack, such eyes!...so innocently wild! So bashfully irresolute! Not a glance but speaks and kindles some thought of love!" (III, i).

In *The School for Scandal*, Careless says:

"That…to me, is as stern a looking rogue as ever I saw; an unforgiving eye" (IV, i).

In *The Critic*, Puff reminds Whiskerandos and Tilburina:

"If you go out without the parting look, you might as well dance out" (II, ii).

Then we have Jane Austen describing the emotional force of the eyes in her novels. In *Sense and Sensibility* Mrs Dashwood says "There was always a something…in Willoughby's eyes at times, which I did not like" (p 338). In *Pride and Prejudice* Sir William interrupts Darcy and Elizabeth as they dance but comments that her "bright eyes are also upbraiding me" (p 92). General Tilney declares to Catherine in *Northanger Abbey* "My eyes will be blinding for the good of others; and yours preparing by rest for future mischief" (p 187). Emma's eyes invited Mr Knightley 'irresistibly to come to her and be thanked' (*E* p 330), while in *Mansfield Park* 'Fanny's eyes followed Edmund, and her heart beat for him…and saw his look' (p 139). In *Persuasion* Jane describes the loving glance of Captain Wentworth's 'half-averted eyes and more than half-expressive glance' (p 185).

Jane's fascination with Sheridan's, *The Rivals*

In *Sense and Sensibility*, Willoughby is referred to as Brandon's 'more fortunate rival' (p 49) while Lucy Steele and Elinor Dashwood are seen as 'the two fair rivals' (p 145). Wickham and Darcy were rivals for Elizabeth Bennet in *Pride and Prejudice*. John Thorpe was a rival for Catherine Morland in *Northanger Abbey*. In *Mansfield Park*, Julia and Maria Bertram were rivals for Henry Crawford during the rehearsals for *Lovers Vows*. In *Emma*, there was a time when Mr Knightley believed Frank Churchill was his rival, and Jane Fairfax believed Emma 'had been a rival' (p 403) for Frank's love. Then in *Persuasion* schemes of Mr Elliot to marry Anne were thwarted and Captain Wentworth won her heart (p 237).

Love and Marriage in *The Rivals* and Jane's novels

The Rivals promotes traditional values and so do Jane's novels where the heroines and heroes journey from attraction to love and marriage. Humour is always an integral ingredient.

Sense and Sensibility: Elinor loves Edward, but his mother insists he marry an heiress. Elinor and her family move to a cottage in Devonshire where she endures many trials before uniting with Edward.

Pride and Prejudice; Elizabeth initially annoyed by the wealthy Darcy's arrogance rejects his proposal of marriage. Later she realizes she has misjudged him and both undergo significant change before they ultimately disclose their love for each other.

Northanger Abbey; The naive Catherine Moreland meets Henry Tilney in Bath. His father General Tilney believing she is an heiress invites her to the Abbey. He sends her away on discovering she is not. Henry's sister Eleanor marries a wealthy man, enabling him to eventually marry Catherine.

Mansfield Park; Fanny, at the age of eleven, leaves Portsmouth to live with her rich cousins, the Bertrams, at *Mansfield Park*. Edmund Bertram becomes her friend but she falls in love with him. Mary Crawford arrives at *Mansfield Park* and Edmund is infatuated with her but she rejects him. Fanny consoles Edmund and they eventually marry.

Emma; Mr Knightley has loved Emma for years but when he was almost lost to her 'It darted through her, with the speed of an arrow, that Mr Knightley must marry no one but herself!' (p 408). He tells her "My dearest Emma…If I loved you less, I might be able to talk about it more…you understand my feelings - and will return them if you can" (p 430).

Persuasion; Anne says in *Persuasion* "All the privilege I claim for my own sex…is that of loving longest, when existence or when hope is gone!" (p 235). She was parted from Captain Wentworth at nineteen. They met again and their love was rekindled 'Her character was now fixed on his mind as perfection itself' (pp 241/2). Later 'Anne gloried in being a sailor's wife' (p 252).

Jane, like Sheridan, is clear sighted about money and its function in marriage

In *The Rivals* Captain Jack Absolute is in love with Lydia but also likes her fortune. Although dealt with humorously, Mrs Bennet's fear in *Pride and Prejudice*, that she and her daughters could be made homeless if her husband should die, is a real one. After Elizabeth rejects Mr Collins' proposal he cruelly reminds her that she may not get another offer. "Your portion is unhappily so small it will...undo the effects of your loveliness" (P 108).

Catherine Morland says in *Northanger Abbey*, "I hate the idea of one great fortune looking out for another...to marry for money I think the wickedest thing in existence" (p 124). Isabella Thorpe discards Catherine's brother on hearing that his income is only £400 a year, and marries the rich Captain Tilney.

Mary Crawford and Edmund Bertram reveal their stark attitudes to money in *Mansfield Park* when she says "A large income is the best recipe for happiness" but on hearing that he intends 'only not to be poor' tells him "I do not...think I shall even respect you" (p 213).

In *Emma*, the well-off heroine of the same name declares "I have none of the usual inducements of women to marry...few married women are half as much mistress of their husband's house, as I am of Hartfield" (E p 84). Meanwhile Jane Fairfax and Frank Churchill keep their engagement a secret until his fortune is secured.

In *Persuasion*, Sir Walter Elliot considers the 'gentleman' curate Mr Wentworth a 'nobody' as he is not a 'man of property' (p 23) and feels that his daughter Anne's marriage to the curate's brother Captain Wentworth would be, 'a very degrading alliance' (p 26).

Inheritance dealings in *The School for Scandal* and *Sense and Sensibility*

Both Sheridan and Austen comment on the greed of human nature and its corrupting influence. As Joseph says in *The School for Scandal* 'Avarice is the vice of age' (v). His scenes are straightforward and comic, while hers are very complex in a story line from *Sense and Sensibility*. In both play and novel, fiscal terminology is used.

Though *The School for Scandal* is set in London's West End, where the Aristocracy and leisured classes live, Sheridan has the new moneyed circle reside in the City of London and banters with their language using terms like, collateral, loan, security, stock and the recent Annuity Bill. This financial jargon has the footman Trip engage in what would be the accepted province of his master with the added joke that his master's fine clothes are his "collateral security" (III,ii). Such humour reflects the increased social mobility of the time. Part of the plot has rich uncle Oliver come from India intending to make his two nephews, the Surface brothers Charles and Joseph his heirs. He needs to know something of their characters, and in the guise of 'Mr. Premium' a money lender, visits Charles first. Charles tells him he needs to borrow money and apart from "a few horses and a 'dev'lish' rich uncle in the East Indies" the only possessions he has are "the family pictures". Sir Oliver listens to Charles relate their history and offers to purchase them all. But Charles refuses to sell one picture because it is of his uncle "poor Noll. The old fellow has been very good to me...and I'll keep his picture while I've a room to put it in" (III,iii). Sir Oliver is delighted with the good-natured Charles who reveals his affection and loyalty for his uncle in this one deed. Sir Oliver then visits Joseph in the guise of 'old Stanley' a penniless relation of his mother. They talk about Joseph's rich 'uncle' and Joseph tells him, "Sir Oliver...what he has done for me has been a mere nothing...A few presents now and then - china, shawls, congou tea, avadavats, and Indian crackers". Sir Oliver (aside) says "Here's gratitude for twelve thousand pounds" and has seen Joseph's corrupt nature (IV, ii). Later he decides that "Charles is my heir" (V, i)

In *Sense and Sensibility*, the outcome is much more serious and Jane shows how quickly the Dashwood family descend into genteel poverty. She highlights the reduced circumstances of Mrs Dashwood and her three daughters who are about to lose their inheritance, because the good intentions of their morally weak step-brother John Dashwood are swept aside by his mean and cunning wife. She subtly blinds her compliant husband and proceeds to erode the rightful inheritance of his step-sisters. Jane extracts humour from this devastating and cruel situation while skilfully exposing the serious plight of women forced to endure genteel poverty.

Mr John Dashwood promised his dying father that he would help his stepmother Mrs Dashwood and his three step-sisters, and decides to give them three thousand pounds, but Mrs John Dashwood does not approve. She persuades him to reduce this amount by half. She then quickly suggests he should only help his step mother, but when he mentions "something of the annuity kind" she frightens him that the mother is "stout...healthy, and hardly forty...An annuity is a very serious business; it comes over and over every year, and there is no getting rid of it" (p 10). Eventually she persuades her husband not to give them any money and they are cheated out of their inheritance.

Then Mrs John Dashwood sets about taking from them the little they have, by laying claim to the china, silver and linen and reducing them to the benefit of 'such kind of neighbourly acts as his own wife pointed out' (p 13). His lack of integrity and her own scheming moral bankruptcy is tightly written by Jane Austen, with a dramatic climax. It goes further than any of the contrivances of Sheridan's characters and deals with matters more sinister and dishonest.

Values of town and country are themes in Sheridan's plays and Jane's novels

Due to the Industrial Revolution, the contrast between town and country values became an increasingly common theme in the play and novel of the 18th Century. Literature generally tended to show townsfolk as shallow while portraying country people with greater moral integrity. Town life entrenched in money and wealth gives rise to scandal. Country life, on the other hand, with its agricultural values, makes for traditional virtues. Sheridan played with this value system in his comic writing and Jane Austen in turn exploits it as a useful means in which to develop decent resolutions to her characters' dilemmas. The action of Sheridan's *The Rivals* takes place in the sophisticated city of Bath, but its heroine Lydia Languish, first met 'Ensign Beverley' in Gloucestershire. Another suitor, Bob Acres, comes to Bath from 'Clod Hall' intending to learn to dance the Cotillon. Although he fails to capture Lydia, it is his countrified good nature and generous gesture which make the end of *The Rivals* into a joyful celebration.

In *The School for Scandal* the young Lady Teazle tells her older husband Sir Peter "though I was educated in the country, I know very well that women of fashion in London are accountable to nobody after they are married" (II, i). He reminds her that when he met her she was 'the daughter of a plain country squire', now she is in danger from the gossip and corruption of London. Yet, Lady Teazle's redeeming quality is her honesty, and as she hides from Sir Peter in the famous 'Screen' scene she learns of his genuine concern for her welfare. She later tells him; "Sir Peter, I do not expect you to credit me, but the tenderness you expressed for me…has penetrated so to my heart" (IV, iii). Their marriage becomes a love match.

In *Sense and Sensibility*, the Dashwood sisters come to stay in the West End of London where both have unhappy experiences. In *Pride and Prejudice* when Darcy remarks that country people "move in a very confined and unvarying society" Mrs Bennet replies "I cannot see that London has any great advantage over the country...except the shops and public places. The country is a vast deal pleasanter" (p 43).

In *Northanger Abbey*, adolescent Catherine is delighted when the Allens take her to Bath but she soon meets depravity in greedy General Tilney. In *Mansfield Park* the Crawfords from London have a corrupting influence on the Bertram family. In *Persuasion*, the vain Sir Walter Elliot, who is in debt, leases his country estate to tenants while he and his daughters live cheaply in Bath. The town and country situation could also be a source for the development of humour, as shown in *Emma* when Mrs Elton 'who wanted to be doing something' is comically revealed to be a nasty snob.

Echoes of Sheridan's blunders in Jane's *Emma*

Sheridan's father wrote a popular play called *Captain O'Blunder*, and in his play *The School for Scandal*, Sheridan has Lady Sneerwell tell Joseph Surface that she was "a fool and idiot, to league with such a blunderer!" (V, iii). Jane once again echoes Sheridan in her novel *Emma* where incidents of "blunder" touch many of the characters. Emma believed she knew 'the secret of everybody's feelings' and 'proposed to arrange everybody's destiny' (pp 412/3). She assumed that Mr Elton was in love with Harriet Smith "through a series of strange blunders!" (p 331) and wrongly believes the cheating Frank Churchill is in love with herself when he is secretly engaged to Jane Fairfax. Frank almost lets their secret out, and later while playing a game of letters he boldly selects the word 'blunder' and 'there was a blush on Jane's cheek which gave it a meaning not otherwise ostensible' (p 348). Finally, truth is revealed and Emma who was a victim of her own vanity is ashamed of 'The blunders, the blindness of her own head and heart!' (pp 411/2).

Gossip, Gossip, Gossip "There's no stopping people's tongues" (*SFS* I, i)

In *The School for Scandal* Sheridan satirises the fascination with gossip while exposing its degenerative power. He parodies fashionable eighteenth century society and promotes a lesson which cuts across time. Gossip, a common feature of social behaviour, can destroy reputations, careers and even marriages. Its corrosive action contaminates both the originator and receiver. Sheridan creates a variety of gossips and uses them to convey its evil outcome. He contrasts the integrity and truth of 'Maria' with the malicious inventions of 'Lady Sneerwell' and her 'school' and the damage wrought by such as Mrs Candour. He lets Sir Peter and Lady Teazle's marriage, not to mention their reputation, come perilously close to being totally wrecked by gossip.

Jane also develops gossipy characters and entertains through humour while touching on profound human issues. The wider scope of the novel allows her to develop the theme of gossip more intricately and she creates a diverse spectrum of characters to illustrate the evils it can foster. In fact it appears that many of Jane's gossips are based on characters from Sheridan's 'school'.

Sheridan's Lady Sneerwell lives on in Lucy Steele (*SS*), in Lady Catherine de Bourgh (*PP*) and in Mrs Norris (*MP*). The character of Caroline Bingley in *Pride and Prejudice* has obvious traces of Mrs Candour. Mrs Jennings in *Sense and Sensibility* and Miss Bates in *Emma*, both create bother through their incessant chatter just like Mrs Candour does. Also in the spectrum is Nurse Rooke of *Persuasion* who brings welcome news and speculation to the bedsides of her patients. And gossips like the cheeky John Thorpe who uses the 'licence of invention' (*SFS* I.i) in *Northanger Abbey* and George Wickham from *Pride and Prejudice*, a 'male slanderer' (*SFS* I.i) are all in Jane's spectrum.

"I tell everybody of it and so does Charlotte" (*SS* p 182)

In *Sense and Sensibility* Colonel Brandon has heard two ladies talking about Willoughby in a stationer's shop in Pall Mall. He hesitantly informs Elinor Dashwood "in a voice so little attempting concealment…The name of Willoughby…first caught my attention…everything was now finally settled respecting his marriage with Miss Grey…as soon as the ceremony was over, they were to go to Combe Magna, his seat in Somersetshire" (p 199). Brandon, a man of integrity, passes on the information with discretion. His careful and caring character is acutely aware of its significance.

While dining at Barton Park, Mrs Jennings, who loves news and gossip, shouts over to Marianne "I have found you out...I know where you spent the morning" (p 67). Elinor, sitting nearby, thus hears that Willoughby had taken Marianne to his aunt's home at Allenham while the aunt was away. Marianne has committed a dangerous breach of etiquette. Although Mrs Jennings is telling the truth her insensitive proclamation hurts Marianne's feelings and exposes her reputation to speculation and gossip. Jane Austen is showing that a seemingly innocent remark can have serious implications.

Later Mrs Jennings is quite openly chatting to Elinor about Marianne and Willoughby and says "Don't we all know it must be a match...and did not I know that your sister came to town with me on purpose to buy wedding clothes?...I tell everybody of it and so does Charlotte" (p 182). Mrs Jennings is letting imagination become fact. Telling of Marianne's 'purpose to buy wedding clothes' is cruelly ironic given that Marianne has already been deserted by Willoughby. To Marianne's distress is now added the embarrassment that everyone is expecting a marriage that will never happen.

Mrs Jennings hears that Willoughby "is to be married very soon...Mrs Taylor told me of it half an hour ago, and she was told it by a particular friend of Miss Grey herself...Well, said I, all I can say is, that if it is true, he has used a young lady of my acquaintance abominably ill" (p 192). Mrs Jennings simply delights in the attention her news and gossip brings but lacks good judgement as to its truth and appears unaware of the impact it might have on others. Despite her love of scandal, her insensitivity and wasted powers of invention, Mrs Jennings values are shown to be in the right place, as she defends Edward Ferrers for "acting like an honest man".

Later, she cannot resist a visit of 'comfort and inquiry' (p 271) to the Steele Sisters, who themselves are scandal mongers. The Steele sisters are disloyal to each other and listen outside doors and would even hide "in a closet or behind a chimney-board" (p 274) to discover each other's secrets. Moreover, Lucy Steele is a ruthless social climber who abandons Edward to marry his richer brother Robert. Her final 'flourish of malice' to hurt Elinor (p 366) would do credit to Sheridan's Lady Sneerwell. Ironically it is Mrs Jennings' prompting Elinor to talk to Miss Steele and "Get it all out of her, my dear" (p 271) that divulges the crucial detail affecting Elinor's future.

Everybody declared...he was the wickedest young man in the world (*PP* p 294)

Jane Bennet in *Pride and Prejudice* like 'Maria' in *The School for Scandal* resists gossip when she refuses to condemn Darcy. She reminds Elizabeth, "I would wish not to be hasty in censuring anyone; but I always speak what I think". Elizabeth replies, "I know you do; and it is that which makes the wonder. With your good sense...to be candid without ostentation or design - to take the good of everybody's character...and say nothing of the bad - belongs to you alone" (pp 14/15). Jane Bennet was 'the only creature' who did not condemn Darcy. When Elizabeth asks Jane if people should be told about Wickham's lies, Jane advises against it saying "The general prejudice against Mr Darcy is so violent, that it would be the death of half the good people in Meryton, to attempt to place him in an amiable light... Wickham will soon be gone...it will not signify to anybody...what he really is" (p 226).

Yet because they do not expose Wickham he goes on to seduce their sister Lydia. Here Jane Austen explores a permutation of gossip where good intentions and good actions can have bad results. It is the willingness of people to believe gossip that allows Darcy's character to be defamed, while making it easier for Wickham to deceive others. While Darcy's intrinsically honest and good hearted nature is concealed by his pride, Wickham's jealous deception is masked by his geniality and charm. Like Sheridan, Jane Austen displays how appearances can deceive.

Wickham exploits the power of gossip to spread his slander with "no scruples in sinking Mr Darcy's character", so that everybody was soon 'pleased to think how much they had always disliked Mr Darcy before they had known anything of the matter' (p 138). Even Elizabeth, is shown to be as gullible as the rest. Jane Austen not only shows how public opinion is quick to change and condemn, but also how it hypocritically attempts disguise of its foolishness.

Once Wickham's wickedness is exposed, they strove 'to blacken the man, who, but three months before, had been almost an angel of light. He was declared to be in debt to every tradesman...and his intrigues, all honoured with the title of seduction, had been extended into every tradesman's family…and everybody…had always distrusted the appearance of his goodness' (pp 294/5). Wickham personifies a statement by Maria in *The School for Scandal* 'I'll not debate how far scandal may be allowable; but in a man…it is always contemptible' (1, i). Jane finally reverses the initial impressions of the characters of Darcy and Wickham. This mirrors Sheridan's strategy in *The School for Scandal* where the characters of Joseph and Charles Surface are similarly reversed.

Caroline Bingley, in the same way as Mrs Candour, tell the truth in a manner guaranteed to denigrate Jane Bennet and further her own interest with Darcy. He listens as she protests "excessive regard" for Jane and wishes "with all my heart she were well settled. But with such a father and mother, and such low connections, I am afraid there is no chance of it" (p 36). Caroline conspires to keep Bingley in London, while she pretends to be Jane's friend, asking her to write and "lessen the pain of separation" (p 116). With a touch of malice, she writes to Jane and tells her that Darcy's sister Georgiana and Bingley should marry for their "relations all wish the connection" (p 118). When Jane visits Caroline in London, she is told by her that Bingley knew she was in town but was 'partial to Miss Darcy' (p 148). Jane however, is not totally deceived for as she writes to Elizabeth, "there is a strong appearance of duplicity in all this" (p 149). Caroline Bingley manipulates the circumstances for her own benefit by economising with the truth by way of gossipy inferences to discourage and hurt Jane as much as possible. Again, her ways are similar to those Mrs Candour would use.

Sheridan has 'Maria' point out in *The School for Scandal*, "in my opinion, those who report such things are equally culpable" (I, i) and this is an aspect which Jane Austen examines. Lady Catherine de Bourgh clearly listens to gossip and travels to Longbourn to confront Elizabeth Bennet. "A report of a most alarming nature, reached me two days ago…that you…Miss Elizabeth Bennet, would…be soon…united to…my own nephew, Mr Darcy. Though I know it must be a scandalous falsehood…I instantly resolved on setting off for this place" (p 353). The paradoxical irony of the situation is that Lady Catherine challenges Elizabeth who unafraid says that if she is his choice "why may not I accept him?" (p 355). When Lady Catherine tells this to Darcy, it alerts him to the fact that Elizabeth is not lost to him. Lady Catherine, therefore by her involvement with gossip brings about that which she most fears, and good comes out of evil in the same way that the conniving gossips of *The School for Scandal* unintentionally unite Sir Peter Teazle and his wife.

"But what do you think we have been talking of? – You?" (*NA* p 96)

In *Northanger Abbey*, the caddish John Thorpe quizzes the naive Catherine Morland about the wealthy, but childless, Mr and Mrs Allen and decides she must be their heiress. Without scruple, and at an opportune moment, he boasts of this lie to the greedy General Tilney. The General invites Catherine to the Abbey intent on securing her as a rich wife for his son. Jane shows that gossip can still have a fortuitous outcome.

The Tragedy of *Mansfield Park*

Jane reaches the zenith of her gossip creations when she takes Sheridan's Lady Sneerwell into her profound *Mansfield Park* and the contemptible Mrs Norris emerges. Mrs Norris lacks wit, humility and is a ruthless, amoral, scheming woman without conscience or feeling. Even so, she has a wide impact on those she meets because of her 'spirit of activity'. She is 'beholden' to Sir Thomas and her sister Lady Bertram, who both allow her a considerable influence on the upbringing of their children. The third sister Mrs Price living in Portsmouth with a large family and a husband, fond of drink, requests help from Sir Thomas and Lady Bertram. She has not spoken to Lady Bertram for years, the culprit been Mrs Norris, who comes up with the idea of "fostering" Fanny, declaring to Sir Thomas, "I am a woman of few words and professions. Do not let us be frightened from a good deed by a trifle...A niece of our's, Sir Thomas...at least of your's, would not grow up in this neighbourhood without many advantages. I don't say she would be so handsome as her cousins...and, though I could never feel for this little girl the hundredth part of the regard I bear your own dear children...Is not she a sister's child? and could I bear to see her want, while I had a bit of bread to give her? My dear Sir Thomas, with all my faults I have a warm heart: and poor as I am, would rather deny myself the necessaries of life, than do an ungenerous thing" (pp 6/7).

There is a total contradiction between the words and actions of Mrs Norris as she does not intend to contribute either time or money to Fanny's upbringing. Mrs Norris, like Joseph Surface in *The School for Scandal*, presents a front to society. 'As far as walking, talking, and contriving reached, she was thoroughly benevolent...nobody knew better how to dictate liberality to others' (p 8). Greedy and covetous in her dealings with both rich and poor, she believed she was 'the most liberal-minded sister and aunt in the world', protesting to Lady Bertram that she is "not one...that spare their own trouble" (pp 8/9). She complained of having to suffer inconvenience in sending her head maid to collect Fanny, yet she 'regaled' the 'credit of being foremost to welcome' her to *Mansfield Park*. Those around her appear self-absorbed and seem oblivious to her discrepancy of word and action. We, the 'audience', alone view her intent to manipulate others, which is cloaked in self-deception, mirroring Sheridan's dramatic flair where illusion and reality are blurred.

She ironically affirms, "There should always be one steady head to superintend so many young ones" (p 141) as she ingratiates herself to be part of the 'action' of the play. When Sir Thomas returns suddenly from Antigua, Mrs Norris should have been conscious-stricken about the moral dangers which the play *Lover's Vows* had exposed the young people to, instead her 'judgement had been so blinded' that her priority was 'to whisk away Mr Rushworth's pink satin cloak' (pp 179/180).

Her double standards are exposed in her relationship to her nieces. She treats Fanny with contempt and treats Maria and Julia with fawning flattery. Eventually Sir Thomas saw that his daughters were selfish and had little 'self-knowledge' and that Mrs Norris did not realise this. Quick to discern faults in others, her zeal to criticize is based on the values of her own interest. Her unpleasant ways have a ruinous effect on those around her. Only Fanny, the target of her evil, escapes with integrity, while the Bertram daughters become victims of what paradoxically appears as Mrs Norris's desire to encourage and please.

Mrs Norris's long monologues reflect her own shallow interests. While Edmund begs his sister Maria not to take part in the theatricals, Mrs Norris continues to talk, "I had been looking about me in the poultry yard...when who should I see but Dick Jackson...with two bits of deal board in his hand, bringing them to father, you may be sure; mother had chanced to send him of a message to father...and as I hate such encroaching people...I said to the boy directly I'll take the boards to your father...The boy looked very silly and turned away...for I believe I might speak pretty sharp...I hate such greediness - so good as your father is to the family, employing the man all the year round" (pp 141/2).

She almost hopes for the worse and the possibilities it might present for her own aggrandisement; Sir Thomas's dangerous trip to Antigua is a comical prod for her to compose long speeches...in the event of 'any fatal catastrophe' (p 34). She encourages a match between the 'perfectly faultless' Maria and Mr Rushworth, 'by every contrivance' and before Sir Thomas could send his consent from Antigua she was 'talking of it everywhere as a matter not to be talked of at present' (p 39). She talks to Mrs Rushworth about the chance of another match between Julia Bertram and Henry Crawford, saying "It is not a settled thing...But I have very little doubt it will be" (p 118). At Sotherton, despite her sense of 'status', she 'was lingering behind in gossip' (p 91) with Mrs Whitaker acquiring gifts for herself.

She shows Fanny no affection nor concern for her welfare. Edmund is angry on hearing that Fanny has spent hours cutting roses and taking them to Mrs Norris's house in the heat of the day. As Mrs Norris contrives to exonerate herself, she reveals her persecution of Fanny more clearly in her lack of sympathy and charity. Fanny's experience of 'the pains of tyranny, ridicule, and neglect' (p 152) is because of Mrs Norris's victimisation. Yet she holds the moral high ground as Mrs Norris rages at her for refusing a part in the play, "I shall think her a very obstinate, ungrateful girl, if she does not do what her aunt and cousins wish...considering who and what she is" (pp 147).

Mrs Norris was conscious of the impropriety of amateur dramatics, but did not want to disappoint the young people she seeks to ingratiate herself with. She becomes oblivious to the real drama taking place at *Mansfield Park*, through the arrival of the Crawfords. Oblivious of her duty of care she was unaware of the threat posed by Henry Crawford. She contrived to exonerate herself, blaming Fanny because if she 'had accepted Mr Crawford this could not have happened' (p 448).

In realising the role played through his default, by the sycophantic Mrs Norris, Sir Thomas arrives at a greater understanding of himself, unfortunately too late for his daughters. He had been, 'foiled by her evasions, disarmed by her flattery' (p 190) and realized that Mrs Norris has no potential for reform and no possibility for growth of self-perception. His own severe character alienated his daughters, who repressed 'their spirits in his presence' (p 463) so their real character remained 'unknown to him'. He wants them to have all the superficial accoutrements of their position, they had the 'understanding and manners, not the disposition' (p 463). Sadly, he is forced to realise that Mrs Norris had been 'an hourly evil'. Eventually she and Maria are sent to 'another country...where, shut up together...their tempers became their mutual punishment' (p 465). Jane Austen banishes them from the 'Garden of Eden' of *Mansfield Park*.

Sheridan presents the moral perspective in *The School for Scandal* with humour and cynicism in contrast to Jane's *Mansfield Park* which has a darker, almost tragic dimension. Mrs Norris's manoeuvrings amuse us but we are viewing an increasing wrongdoing, the results of not abiding by principle. Fanny is the only one who examines her conscience and it is an active redemptive force for good whereas the others deny, ignore or neglect it, eroding integrity and diminishing the quality of existence. Sir Thomas and Lady Bertram don't set out to be evil but they neglect to see that good is done. Lady Bertram allowed Mrs Norris 'the charge' (p 35) of her children, culpably neglecting them herself. Her concern on Fanny's arrival, was that she would "not tease my poor pug" (p 10) and when Fanny was to live with Mrs Norris, Lady Bertram remarks indifferently "It can make very little difference to you, whether you are in one house or the other" (p 25).

In *Mansfield Park*, 'acting' depicts concern with appearances. All the characters show moral flaws at some point, while Fanny is always true to herself and never "acts" for her own gain. Jane, like Sheridan plays with paradox, as Fanny tells a profound truth when she says "No, indeed, I cannot act" (p 145). She truly feels while the others often 'act' feelings for the sake of appearance, for gain or to be nice. Fanny knows herself.

Edmund errs with the theatricals and fails to see the lack of morality in Mary Crawford, believing her faults are 'of principle' (p 456). Yet he came close to losing his piety with her. He is 'saved' because he is not "an advocate for marriage without love" (pp 346/347). In accordance with the nature of redeeming love, and romance too, as in Sheridan's drama, he and Fanny become the perfect couple.

Sir Thomas does get some reward in that his niece Fanny operates as a force for good. His daughters, and son Tom, break the moral code by not honouring their parents. The inebriate gluttony of Tom, who wastes his brother's inheritance and the lust of the daughters' flirtations with Henry Crawford and the greed of their hapless marriages indicate errors of judgement. Yet these errors are forgivable if accompanied with regret or remorse. Tom Bertram, 'had suffered and he had learnt to think' (p 462) and he rebuked himself for his sister's adultery partly blaming 'the dangerous intimacy of his unjustifiable theatre' (p 462).

Fanny is the chief redemptive force in *Mansfield Park* and her goodness contrasts with others and the attractive but corrupt "incomers" Mary and Henry Crawford. Also, Jane Austen plays with appearance and reality as Sheridan did. Fanny has a weak body but strong moral core, whereas Mary Crawford is physically robust but morally weak. Fanny stays true to principle. Mary lives with regret. Fanny is brought up in poverty with 'degenerate' parents, but she emerges sound and steadfast despite such a tough start in life. This is in contrast to the Bertram sisters who had the best education. So, what point is Jane Austen making, where does principle come from? Is redemption by the grace of God? Henry Crawford a "most horrible flirt" (p 43) toys with the feelings of Maria and Julia Bertram. When he sets out to make Fanny love him, he brags openly of his love for her to his sisters, to Sir Thomas as 'it would be rather gratifying...to have enlightened witnesses of the progress of his success' (p 332). This clearly links him to Sheridan's character Joseph Surface.

During rehearsals, attractive Mary Crawford asks "What gentleman among you am I to have the pleasure of making love to?" (p 143) revealing her wanton flirtatious manner. She has a kinder side to her nature though. She looked 'with astonished eyes at Mrs Norris' as she cruelly raged at Fanny (p 147). Mary comforts Fanny. Later she writes to Fanny at Portsmouth "A most scandalous...rumour has just reached me, and...dear Fanny... Henry is blameless...in spite of a moment's etourderie thinks of nobody but you…I am sure it will be all hushed up' (p 437). Mary, who is a Lady Sneerwell type, has her own and Henry's best interests in mind. Soon Fanny reads in a newspaper of "a matrimonial fracas…of Wimpole Street; the beautiful Mrs R… having quitted her husband's roof in company with the well-known and captivating Mr C the intimate friend…of Mr R" (p 440).

Sheridan points out the evils and dangers of gossip, whether containing some truth or not, for its victims and perpetrators while exploiting its humorous potential for the stage. As Jane embraces his theme, given the wider scope of the novel, she shows the unpleasant consequences that ensue and the element of suffering involved. In the sad exile from home of Maria Bertram, is mapped out a future where she will never be allowed to escape from a life of shame and regret. The audience and readers of Sheridan and Austen may have learnt from the truths uncovered, but it is not certain that all their characters have. In *Mansfield Park* Jane makes room for doubt and regret, evoking the passage of time and damaged lives outside the carefree orbit of the ideal couple.

"Highbury gossips! - Tiresome wretches" (*Emma* pg.58)

Jane's acute observations are developed succinctly very early in her next great novel *Emma* where attention is drawn to the talkative nature of the residents of Highbury with their "tittle-tattle" (p 56). Emma herself voices to Mr Knightley "Highbury gossips! - Tiresome wretches!" (p 58). Even that bastion of integrity, Mr Knightley cannot resist sharing news with Emma, "I have a piece of news for you. You like news" (p 172). As they talk Miss Bates arrives and launches straight in with "Oh! My dear sir, how are you this morning? My dear Miss Woodhouse…Have you heard the news? Mr Elton is going to be married" (pp 172/173).

Miss Bates of little means, who cares for her elderly mother, is the pivot of gossip in Highbury, her main excitement being the transmission of news. She tends to chatter incessantly about the inconsequential and serious with equal force. She unwittingly provides key information and acts as a catalyst in bringing about Emma's self-realisation and a happy resolution for her. Emma who loves "news" herself, tends to be intolerant of Miss Bates's chatter and during a picnic party at Box hill makes a cruel comment at her expense. Later, Mr Knightley confronts her "How could you be so insolent…to a woman of her character, age, and situation?" (p 374). Emma who had applied her superior wit at the expense of a vulnerable Miss Bates, is now humbled and ashamed of her conduct and begins to redeem herself.

When Mr Perry's plans for a carriage became known, Miss Bates accepts that she may have spread the rumour saying "I must acknowledge, that there was such an idea last spring; for Mrs Perry herself mentioned it to my mother…I am not like Jane…she never betrayed the least thing in the world. Where is she? - Oh! Just behind" (p 346). The irony is that Miss Bates is acutely aware of her own faults, but not of the faults of the real culprit, her niece Jane Fairfax who had written of it to Frank Churchill.

Miss Bates's gossiping is vital to the story line and perhaps the only pleasure in her life. Yet she is also useful in spreading good news. When Mr Knightley and Emma told Mr and Mrs Weston of their wedding plans, Mr Weston hurried to tell Jane Fairfax, who happened to be with Miss Bates and 'it passed…to Mrs Cole, Mrs Perry and Mrs Elton…soon it would be over Highbury…as the evening wonder in many a family circle' (p 468). Here are shades of Mrs Clackitt from *The School for Scandal*. Snake says to Lady Sneerwell, "In the common course of things…it must reach Mrs Clackitt's ears within four-and twenty hours; and… the business is as good as done" (*SFS* I, i).

"tell all to Lady Russell" (*Persuasion* p211)

In *Persuasion*, Jane's last novel, the gossip seems to have a rambling quality, and not meaningful to the story at times. Nurse Rooke frequently visits her patient Mrs Smith who is a friend of Anne Elliot. Mrs Smith tells Anne, "Everybody's heart is open… when they have recently escaped from severe pain, or are recovering the blessing of health, and nurse Rooke…intelligent, sensible woman…has a fund of good sense…Call it gossip…she is sure to have something to relate that is entertaining and profitable" (p 155). Anne comments "A sick chamber may often furnish the worth of volumes" (p 156).

Anne visits Mrs Smith who seems to believe she is to marry Mr Elliot. Mrs Smith heard it from nurse Rooke who "had it from Mrs Wallis…She sat an hour with me…and gave me the whole history" (p

197). Anne laughed saying "She could not make a very long history...of one such little article of unfounded news" (p 197/8). Mrs Smith continues "I think you ought to be made acquainted with Mr Elliot's real character. (pp 198/9). She shocks Anne in her portrait of him as "a man without heart or conscience...He was the intimate friend of my dear husband, who trusted and loved him" (p 199). She tells Anne that at nineteen Mr Elliot married for money "I have often heard him declare, that if baronetcies were saleable, anybody should have his for fifty pounds" (p 202). She then shows Anne a letter she received from Mr Elliot previously in which he writes "I have got rid of Sir Walter and Miss. They are gone back to Kellynch" (p 203). She continues "I have shewn you Mr Elliot, as he was...He is no hypocrite now. He truly wants to marry you...It does not come to me in quite so direct a line...Mr Elliot talks...to Colonel's very pretty silly wife...repeats it all to her nurse...brings it all to me" (pp 204/5). Anne comments to Mrs Smith "Facts or opinions which are to pass through the hands of so many...can hardly have much truth left" (p 205). Anne's comment and Mrs Smith's chatter can be compared to a scene from *The School for Scandal* between Mrs Candour and Maria;

Mrs Candour. People will talk- there's no preventing it. Why it was but yesterday I was told that Miss Gadabout had eloped with Sir Filigree Flirt. But, Lord! there's no minding what one hears; though, to be sure I had this from very good authority.

Maria. Such reports are highly scandalous.

Mrs Candour. So they are, child - shameful...the world is so censorious, no character escapes...who would have suspected your friend, Miss Prim of an indiscretion!...they say her uncle stopped her last week, just as she was stepping into the York Mail with her dancing-master.

Maria. I'll answer for't there are no grounds for that report.

Mrs Candour. Oh, no foundation in the world...No more probably than for the story circulated last month of Mrs Festino's affair with Colonel Cassino...

Joseph. The licence of invention some people take is monstrous indeed.

Maria. 'Tis so - but in my opinion those who report such things are equally culpable. (I,i)

When Mrs Smith gives Anne 'full liberty' to tell all to Lady Russell (p 211) the reader like Anne, speculates where truth might lie. Is this plethora of gossip the consolation of the lonely woman in a sick bed? Is Mr Elliot's past revealed to discredit or highlight his reformed conduct? The reader decides. The famous screen scene in Sheridan's *The School for Scandal* (1V, iii) comes to mind once again where the audience is invited to form its own opinion. Jane gives her readers a similar illusion of autonomy.

Jane Austen and Sheridan show that the listener can be corrupted by the act of listening itself, and the alternative is to avoid or "silence" the speaker. Idle speculation can escalate to malicious invention or even the very truth itself can be damaging. We are entertained by gossip, and can be guilty by association.

A little bit of Art in Sheridan and Austen

Sheridan's *The School for Scandal* features an emotional scene where Charles refuses to sell his Uncle's portrait and reveals his basic good nature (IV, i). Jane follows Sheridan, and in each novel has an episode on either paintings or miniatures. For example, in *Pride and Prejudice* 'In the gallery…Elizabeth walked on in quest of the only face whose features would be known to her' (P 250). Emma Woodhouse liked to paint and 'Her many beginnings were displayed. Miniatures, half-lengths whole- lengths, pencil, crayon, and watercolours…all tried in turn' (*E* p 44).

A sense of the ridiculous

Returning to Sheridan's *The Critic*, where Sir Fretful Plagiary declares to Sneer, "He might take out some of the best things in my tragedy and put them into his own comedy" (*The Critic* 1, i) this is what Jane did. One example is *Persuasion* where Jane sends up a "frightful day" at Lyme when the report of Louisa Musgrave's fall 'had spread among the workmen and boatmen about the Cobb, and many were collected near them…at any rate, to enjoy the sight of a dead young lady, nay, two dead young ladies for it proved twice as fine as the first report' (p 111).

Puff's phrase in *The Critic* "Where they do agree on the stage, their unanimity is wonderful!" (II, ii) is shared with Mrs Elton in *Emma* "where the waters do agree, it is quite wonderful the relief they give" (p 275).

His one-dimensional characters are universal types, so are Jane's three dimensional characters. Just like Sheridan, she wrote about humanity with all its faults.

Sheridan lived life on the grand scale, flamboyantly achieving national acclaim but also facing desolation with bravado and courage. The Prince Regent told Napoleon's ambassador that Sheridan "is the most extraordinary creature alive...endowed with the rarest talents". In 1804 the Prince wrote to Sheridan, "No one in the world entertains a higher regard for you...I may even say entertains a sincere affection for you that I do". Enjoying the party lifestyle and drinking copiously, Sheridan neglected his wife Elizabeth which encouraged her affair with Lord Edward Fitzgerald by whom she had a daughter in 1792. Within a year, Elizabeth had died and was followed shortly by the death of the infant who Sheridan had taken to be looked after as his own. His remorse and sadness is attested by contemporary accounts. In 1795, Sheridan married 'Hecca' the daughter of the Dean of Winchester and they had one son born in 1796. His affairs continued and most spectacularly he was intrigued romantically, since the early 1780's, by Lady Bessborough, younger sister of Georgiana, Duchess of Devonshire and was very much in love with her until his death.

Sheridan "had not a tinge of malice" (Gibbon). He was an idealist but his politics were of the future and even though in his theatre he entertained the appearance of frivolity, he was deadly serious, appreciating the implications of social realities. He was possibly the most charismatic character of his generation with his great theatrical triumphs and later his oratorical flair at Parliament. Everything he accomplished was linked to his astonishing linguistic brilliance making even his personal flaws part of an engaging charm.

From her childhood, Jane had learnt from the established playwright who in turn came to value and declare her writing as one of the "cleverest things he ever read". Both were blessed with the gift of eloquence. Both played with ideas and illusions of 'surface' where appearances mask reality. A reflection in the paradox of their lives, where a country Tory clergyman's daughter would appear to have little to connect her to a flamboyant Whig personality, yet each transcended the manners of their time, with a psychological resonance and humour which continues to inform and entertain today as a benchmark of literary empathy and excellence.

CHAPTER 10

ROMANCE OF JANE AND TOM

It was Christmas time in Hampshire,1795. A young Irishman, Tom Lefroy had come from Ireland to spend the holidays with his Uncle, the Reverend George Lefroy, at the Rectory of Ashe a few miles north of the Austen's home in Steventon. Jane was very friendly with the Reverend's wife, "Madame" Lefroy, and was soon introduced to the handsome stranger.

For Jane and Tom it was love at first sight, but their brief courtship lasted only four weeks before they were parted never to meet again. For Jane, the idyllic dream was over, but the heartache haunted all her novels. Shortly before he died Tom Lefroy admitted to his nephew, Thomas Edward Preston Lefroy, that he had a "boyish love for Jane". A "boyish love" is a young love but is nevertheless love.

Two letters, written by Jane to Cassandra in January 1796, reveal her daring conduct with her "Irish friend" during the Christmas season and the New Year of 1795/1796.

'My Dear Cassandra,

In the first place I hope you will live twenty-three years longer. Mr. Tom Lefroy's birthday was yesterday, so that you are very near of an age. After this necessary preamble I shall proceed to inform you that we had an exceeding good ball last night. ...We were so terrible good as to take James in our carriage but indeed he deserves encouragement for the very great improvement which has lately taken place in his dancing. Miss Heathcote is pretty, but not near so handsome as I expected. Mr. H. began with Elizabeth, and afterwards danced with her again; but they do not know how to be particular. I flatter myself, however, that they will profit by the three successive lessons which I have given them.

You scold me so much in the nice long letter which I have this moment received from you, that I am almost afraid to tell you how my Irish friend and I behaved. Imagine to yourself everything most profligate and shocking in the way of dancing and sitting down together, I can expose myself, however, only once more, because he leaves the country soon after next Friday, on which day we are to have a dance at Ashe after all. He is a very gentleman like, good-looking, pleasant young man, I assure you. But as to our having ever met, except at the three last balls, I cannot say much; for he is so excessively laughed at about me at Ashe, that he is ashamed of coming to Steventon, and ran away when we called on Mrs. Lefroy a few days ago...

...We had a visit yesterday morning from Mr. Benjamin Portal, whose eyes are as handsome as ever. Everybody is extremely anxious for your return, but as you cannot come home by the Ashe ball, I am glad that I have not fed them with false hopes. James danced with Alethea, and cut up the turkey last night with great perseverance...I wish Charles had been at Manydown, because he would have given you some description of my friend, and I think you must be impatient to hear something about him...After I had written the above, we received a visit from Mr. Tom Lefroy and his cousin George. The latter is really very well-behaved now; and as for the other, he has but one fault, which time will, I trust, entirely remove - it is that his morning coat is a great deal too light. He is a very great admirer of Tom Jones, and therefore wears the same coloured clothes, I imagine, which he did when he was wounded...

I condole with Miss M. on her losses and with Eliza on her gains, and am ever yours,

J.A.

Here, Jane gives us a genuine glimpse of her youthful behaviour when her sister was not around to restrain her. Writing so explicitly to Cassandra displays evidence of the great trust they had in each other. What if this letter had fallen into others' hands? Jane Austen was courageous in even posting it, or was she reaching out to Cassandra for comfort? The letter is one of two to survive and its survival must have been a mistake. Caroline Austen, niece of Jane and Cassandra, wrote that Cassandra burnt most of Jane's letters '2 or 3 years before her own death'. (*My Aunt Jane Austen, A Memoir* p 10).

The reality of Jane and Tom's romance can only be imagined. It also shows that the young Jane Austen was a real romantic and in search of love. Jane opens her heart in the letter to Cassandra, who since October, had been staying with her intended in-laws, the Fowles, at Kingsbury in Berkshire. Cassandra was engaged to their son Tom who was now serving as chaplain to the Earl of Cravan's regiment in the West Indies. The sauciness of Jane's letter must have worried Cassandra who understood her sister's nature. She was not there to curb Jane's youthful excesses, and as Jane wrote "the nice long letter which I have this moment received from you, that I am almost afraid to tell you how my Irish friend and I behaved" did not help.

Three weeks before, Jane was happy to enjoy all the attention of the young men at the balls and dances in the neighbourhood. Then the dashing Irishman came into her life. Perhaps it was her turn to fall in love. After all, she was one of the bridesmaids to her cousin Jane Cooper when she married Captain Thomas Williams in 1792. Also, soon her sister Cassandra would be leaving Steventon to marry Tom Fowle once he returned from the West Indies. Cassandra usually curbed Jane's over eagerness on occasions (it was said) when she would flirt too much, and regarded Jane's flirtations with trepidation. She must have been shocked and worried on reading that Jane showed off too much by pursuing Tom in the public gaze, and by writing of her flirting as if it was a drama. It seemed although Jane was clever and bright her emotions were too strong and her experience too little.

There was nobody there for Jane to confide in. Her brothers, James (now the Curate of nearby Deane); and Henry (back from military duty), were around, but did not intervene. Henry had a friend with him, John Warren, who had parted from the Austens at Deane Gate to go to town. After the ball, Henry would soon return to Oxford, and from there on to the Regiment in Chelmsford. More visitors were arriving at Steventon in a few days, but it was just Jane, her mother and father who were staying in the Steventon Rectory that Christmas of 1795.

The meeting between Jane and Tom, two intelligent young people, may also have been a meeting of minds. Tom (Thomas Langlois) Lefroy was born in County Limerick, Ireland on the 8th of January 1776. He was the sixth child and first son in a family of twelve. His father, Anthony Lefroy of Carrickglass (Cartilages) Co. Longford was for a time a Colonel in the army, and hailed from a Huguenot family which had sought refuge in England in the 16th Century. His mother's name was Anne Gardiner, and it seems that this marriage was not a happy one. Tom was a student from November 1790 at Trinity College, Dublin, and graduated with a Bachelor of Arts degree in 1795. He was a brilliant student, winning many university prizes and medals. Another student of that time was Thomas Moore, the Irish composer, and some years before, Wolfe Tone, the Irish patriot had studied there. Members of the Ascendancy and wealthy Protestants sent their sons to Trinity college, where standards were on a par with the universities of Oxford and Cambridge. Oliver Goldsmith and Edmund Burke, were educated there, as were many leading members of Parliament.

Tom celebrated his 20th birthday in January 1796 before he left Ashe for London. The Lefroy family expected him to do well and marry 'money'. According to his great-uncle, Benjamin Langlois who had financed his education, he had a 'good heart, a good mind, good sense and as little to correct in him as ever I saw in one of his age'. His lifestyle in Ireland would have been Spartan, and he must have embraced the party season in Hampshire and the love of Jane Austen with all the released feeling of his being.

Jane at 20 was described as tall, slim with 'a light step'. She had a pretty face with bright hazel eyes which were 'joyous and intelligent with a lively gaze on the world'. The only known sketch of her to survive captures this distinctive feature wonderfully. Her voice was sweet and a pleasure to listen to, as Tom Lefroy would have discovered. He was different from the usual young men she knew around the neighbourhood, his charm and Irish brogue adding to his attraction. It is not known whether they only met at 'three balls' as Jane wrote to Cassandra, but she must have felt assured that 'cupid' was on her side as Tom was the nephew of her great friend Madame Lefroy. Madame Lefroy was cultured and sophisticated and often accompanied Jane to dances. On occasions they would play music together at house parties, where a piano or harp, flutes and whistles were at hand. Tom Lefroy may have enjoyed these "sessions" during the festivities in Hampshire.

For Jane and Tom that first encounter around Christmas was magical. Jane lived for the moment when she would see him again. From the comings and goings to the balls, there may have been opportunities for Jane and Tom to meet in the lanes of Hampshire, to walk side by side knowing they would soon be close together at the dance. After the dance they would walk with the homeward party in the moonlight still close together for a little while longer. They could not have met in church, as she would remain at Steventon for her father's service and he would remain at Ashe for his uncle's service. Madame Lefroy would tease Tom about Jane, but who was at Steventon for Jane? Her father was there and he would have noticed her elation and happiness, but she needed the down-to-earth Cassandra to be with her.

Jane talked about the novel, *Tom Jones,* with Tom, and as he admired her openness, he may have been a little shocked. They would have discussed his ambitions for the future which would furnish Jane with insights into contemporary Irish affairs 'ere time transfigured' them. Although Jane and Tom were rarely alone together, the short time they shared must have been all the more precious. During that Christmas season, they lived for the moment, walking, stopping, swapping stories, opinions, drinking in that first gulp of love, a love they thought would never end. This love had shades of *Romeo and Juliet.* Was it "Too flattering sweet to be substantial"? (R & J 11, ii).

Jane wanted the world to know of her love for this wonderful Irishman. She writes to Cassandra "imagine to yourself everything most profligate and shocking in the way of dancing and sitting down together". Poor Jane dared all, and by the second ball about the 3rd of January given by the Harwoods at Deane House Jane and Tom drew attention to themselves with their unrestrained and risqué behaviour. Her letter to Cassandra reveals the irony that everyone else was aware of Jane's imprudence but herself. She was too quickly won just like Juliet "I am too fond therefore I should have been more strange I must confess" (R & J 11, ii).

Tom, on his part, was flattered by her attention. She was probably the first English girl he had a chance to get to know and was swept along in a great wave of emotion. At that second ball they were reunited after some days apart but the vigilant Cassandra was not there to calm the situation. Madame Lefroy saw what was happening and realised that this was not one of Jane's girlish flirtations, but much more serious. She remembered just before the second ball she had teased Tom about Jane, and was amused to see him run away when Jane called to see them. Now though, Tom talked about Jane and was very eager to go and visit the Austens at Steventon.

The map of the area around Steventon shows that Deane Gate is at the crossroads where the road from Ashe and the road from Steventon meet. It is likely that the Lefroys and the Austens met and together walked to Deane House, allowing Jane and Tom precious moments together. After the ball, it is possible that the two parties walked home part of the way together, and Jane and Tom had the opportunity to stay close to each other and had "night's cloak" to hide them. (R & J 11, ii).

The third ball was to be held on the 10th January 1796, at the home of Jane's friends the Bigg Withers' in their beautiful house, Manydown, just a few miles west of Steventon. Again, the two parties may have met at Deane Gate and proceeded to Manydown. The happiest time the young lovers spent together was probably at this ball, and Jane let the world at Manydown know it that night. She was once again "particular" in a way Elizabeth and Mr. H. did "not know how to be particular. I flatter myself, however, that they will profit by the three successive lessons which I have given them", she wrote to Cassandra later. Was she "too bold, too reckless"? Would her behaviour end in disaster or would she and Tom exchange faithful vows of love for each other? As they walked home through the woods around Steventon that night, parting was such "sweet sorrow" (R & J 11, ii) They must have accompanied each other as far as the gate at Deane, their parting gate. It is possible they walked together towards Steventon and walked back towards the crossroads, going backwards and forwards many times, speaking words of endearment. Before parting they would have talked about the forthcoming ball at Ashe, where Tom would celebrate his 20th Birthday. But nothing they believed, could surpass their happiness on the night of the Manydown ball, the third ball they were together at. Jane was daring and Tom was daring, and next day the infatuated Tom paid a visit to Steventon, "And what love can do that dares love attempt". (R & J 11, ii)

As Jane tells Cassandra in her letter, that when she visited Mrs. Lefroy at Ashe, Tom ran away, "for he is so excessively laughed at about me, that he is ashamed of coming to Steventon". Tom was a very shy, inexperienced young man. Yet before Jane sends her letter to Cassandra she had something more to tell, "After I had written the above, we received a visit from Mr Tom Lefroy and his cousin George" and two more interesting comments "he has but one fault, which time will, I trust, entirely remove - it is that his morning coat is a great deal too light. He is a very great admirer of the novel *Tom Jones*, and therefore wears the same coloured clothes, I imagine, which he did when he was wounded". So, Tom visits Jane on the day after the Manydown ball, and this showed that he was a gentleman as at that time it was the custom for a gentleman to call to a lady after a ball. This visit raised Jane's hopes of a favourable outcome at the forthcoming dance at Ashe which Mrs. Lefroy was to give for Tom's birthday, before he departed to resume his studies in London. Jane may have walked with Tom and George back towards the Gate at Deane which decided their fate.

Now Jane was very much in love, and all her dancing partners, the boys she once flirted with, saw it too. They wondered whether Jane was becoming too familiar with this Irishman. This Jane was not the Jane Austen they knew. Just like Jane and Tom, they were respectable, well behaved young people. Jane was acting out of character, stepping out of line, but Tom did not know the customs of the Hampshire folk, therefore he went along with Jane.

She writes to Cassandra on Thursday 14th January 1796, the day before the dance at Ashe, (Lt 2)

"Our party to Ashe tomorrow night will consist of Edward Cooper, James…Buller who is now staying with us…I look forward with great impatience to it as I rather expect to receive an offer from my friend in the course of the evening. I shall refuse him, however, unless he promises to give away his white coat…

Tell Mary that I make over Mr Heartley and all his estate to her for her sole use…and…all my other admirers into the bargain wherever she can find them, even the kiss which C. Powlett wanted to give me, as I mean to confine myself in future to Mr Tom Lefroy, for whom I do not care sixpence. Assure her also, proof of Warren's indifference to me, that he actually drew that gentleman's picture for me, and delivered it to me without a sigh.

Friday, - At length the day is come on which I am to flirt my last with Tom Lefroy, and when you receive this it will be over. My tears flow as I write at the melancholy idea..."

Jane shed tears the evening before the dance, but she still believed in a happy ending for her and Tom. She said she did not need any of her admirers any more. In her heart she expected Tom Lefroy to propose. Perhaps she had a feeling of danger, for when she heard the news, whether at Ashe or Steventon or Deane, she was devastated. Tom was being sent to London immediately, and she would see him at Ashe tomorrow night for the last time.

On that starry Friday night, on the 15th January 1796 as Jane and the others headed for the Ashe dance, her thoughts centred on Tom. She had not yet woken up from her dream, she loved him and thought he loved her. Would he ask her to wait for him? Perhaps when he went to London, he would tell his family, and maybe they would agree to a marriage after he finished his studies. She wished Tom would say something to her but he did not. Things were falling apart. Jane Austen must have looked so pretty that night; the young men of the neighbourhood thought so. So, did the young women, but were they sympathetic? Her exuberance over the past few weeks must have amazed them. She and Tom stayed close to each other at the dance. Jane hinted that they might see each other in London. He might have said to her that he would remember her forever, but nothing more. The drama was unfolding under the lights of the drawing room at Ashe in view of all present. Jane kept up a defiant façade, and Tom went along with it. The music played on, they danced feeling more reckless. Faces passed by, Madame Lefroy's especially. In the heat of the night goodbyes were said, good luck was wished to Tom. Jane must have stood there thinking tonight would not be 'sweet sorrow' but bitter sorrow. (R & J 11, ii)

We don't know if Tom walked with Jane to the crossroads near the gate at Deane that night. Perhaps he wanted to speak his mind and open his heart to her but dared not. "By yonder blessed moon I swear" but the moon was "inconstant" (R & J 11, ii). The young lovers were at the mercy of fate, about to embrace their separate destinies, "Night's candles are burnt out" (R & J 111, v). Tom's short spell of freedom was over.

Jane and Tom, both twenty, had the same set of values and would not have departed from them. In her hurt and sadness, Jane thought her great friend Madame Lefroy would help. Madame Lefroy had brought them together, surely she could save them. But Madame Lefroy did nothing. She was not the cruel and wicked aunt of Tom, but it was said that when she realised the position between him and Jane she was alarmed, and she may have been upset at their behaviour. She could not let it carry on, she had to make a decision, so she acted ruthlessly and removed Tom promptly. She was angry with him, how could he string a girl like Jane on? He could not hope to marry her. His father expected great things of his eldest son. A girl like Jane without money, or position was not considered a suitable choice for the Lefroys. Her family had some connections but not enough for Tom's ambitious family. The die was cast. Jane's pain would be swift. The young lovers were parted, "Violent delights… have violent ends" (R & J 11, vi).

It is very fortunate that these two letters from Jane to Cassandra survive. They give us a glimpse of those most important weeks in the life of the young Jane Austen and Tom Lefroy and the young people of Steventon, Ashe, Deane and Manydown. There was Warren who danced with her and who returned to Steventon and presented her with a portrait of Tom Lefroy. This is very significant to the romance, as she probably told Warren that she liked Tom which prompted him to present this surprise gift to her. Jane had now an image of Tom, perhaps the only one of a boyfriend in her possession.

Jane and Tom had just four weeks together before he was banished to London. They never saw each other again. For Jane, it was a "prodigious birth of love" (R & J 1, v) and a prodigious end also. She remembered how they had loved, and laughed, with no thought for the future, ill-fated ill-starred lovers. Tom caused her pain, humiliation and shattered her ego. She was left to her grief, with a broken heart. She would never know if he would have married her if she had a dowry. There was no consolation for her; "shut the door; and when thou has done so, Come weep with me, past hope, past cure, past help". (R & J 1V, i)

Spring came, but Tom Lefroy did not contact Jane again. Cassandra was not there to console her. There was her practical minded mother who may have noticed that Jane was quiet. We know that Mrs Austen remarked one day that Cassandra would be in Berkshire with Tom Fowles but 'the lord knows where Jane will end up'. Jane had her sympathetic father, who knew his daughter was suffering. They had always been close. He would watch out for her and he did.

Her lament for Tom was like a bereavement, yet she reveals an abiding interest in his actions and accomplishments long after their association ended. The old adage comes to mind 'love for a man is a thing apart, for a woman her whole existence'. Tom Lefroy did come back to Hampshire but he did not, or was prevented from going to Steventon, and so did not see Jane. In a letter to Cassandra dated November 1798, nearly three years since Jane and Tom had said goodbye, she writes, "Mrs. Lefroy did come last Wednesday…I was enough alone to hear all that was interesting, which you will easily credit when I tell you that of her nephew she said nothing at all, and of her friend very little. She did not once mention the name of the former to me, and I was too proud to make any enquiries; but on my father afterwards asking where he was, I learnt that he was gone back to London on his way to Ireland, where he is called to the Bar and means to practise" (Lt 11).

So Madame Lefroy, Jane's great friend, could not bring herself to talk about Tom to her. Did she keep him deliberately away from the Austens, just in case that spark with Jane would be rekindled once again. Jane heard the ultimate news that would put an end to any hope she had kept alive throughout the years, for in 1799 Tom married Mary Paul an heiress from County Wexford.

At the age of 23, Jane, a romantic, faced harsh reality and her wounded love remained. There was one certainty, which her life, letters, and novels, reveal, that is she would only marry for love. Marrying for money was abhorrent to her and it would be immoral. Jane had gambled with love and lost and we are the winners. She found refuge in her pen at her small mahogany writing desk and her response was an outpouring of literary genius. Her heart had found its way. She was set on the path to immortality, not through the love of a man but through the love of 'words'.

Her natural wit and her taste for comedy surfaced, and interestingly in all her novels the heroine, after some hurdles, is married to the man she loves. Even in the unfinished *The Watsons*

(1803) Emma turns down a prince because she does not love him. Within three years after her romantic encounter Jane had completed the first drafts of *Sense and Sensibility*, *Pride and Prejudice*, and *Northanger Abbey*. Jane's inner battle on issues of love remained. In *Sense and Sensibility* there is a scene which might echo her romance with Tom Lefroy, and afterwards Cassandra's concern;

"Engagement!" cried Marianne "there has been no engagement."

"No engagement?"

"No, he is not so unworthy as you believe him. He has broken no faith with me."

"But he told you that he loved you?"

"Yes - no - never absolutely…Sometimes I thought it had been - but it never was" (*SS* p 186).

From now on she must not expect life to go her way and for a long time Steventon and its neighbourhood seemed dull to her, as did meeting the same young men she had known before she met Tom. Within a year her sister Cassandra suffered a terrible loss when Tom Fowle was killed in the West Indies. Cassandra never married and lived at home for the remainder of her life. She was not only Jane's sister but her confidant and best friend (Lts p 513/4).

Jane received a proposal of marriage in 1802 when she and Cassandra went to stay with their friends Alethea and Catherine Bigg-Wither and their brother Harris at Manydown. Harris, home from Oxford, asked Jane to marry him on the evening of December 2nd. She accepted, the sisters were delighted, but during the dark night of the soul Jane realized she had made a terrible mistake. In the morning, she and Cassandra left the house in haste. Harris married soon after, and became the father of ten children.

Much of Jane and Tom's short time together was spent dancing at the local house balls. One song in her music collection is called *Nobody loves like an Irishman*, perhaps a cynical reminder to her of the way Tom left her. Jane accepted her situation, but was she ever resigned to it? 'What are men to rocks and mountains?' she wrote in *Pride and Prejudice* (p 154.) Jane heard from time to time about the

'Irish Lefroys'. In 1798 she wrote to Cassandra that the third Miss Irish Lefroy (Tom's sister Sarah) was going to be married (Lt 14) and then wrote no more of them. Many years later in November 1814 Jane's niece Anna Austen at the age of twenty married Ben Lefroy, Madame Lefroy's youngest son (*A History of Jane Austen's Family*) and so fused the DNA of the Austen and Lefroy families. Their daughter Jemima Lefroy was born in 1815, the year when Jane Austen was enjoying the success of her fourth novel, *Emma*.

Yet there is more to the Austen and Lefroy story. Apparently upon learning of Jane's death (18th July 1817) Tom travelled from Ireland to England to pay his respects to the Austen family. Also, nearly thirty years later in 1846 Jemima, was united in marriage to an Irish Lefroy T.E.P. (Thomas Edward Preston) and he was the nephew of Tom Lefroy. So the great niece of Jane Austen married the nephew of Tom Lefroy.

Twenty years later shortly before Tom Lefroy died in 1869 this nephew asked his uncle about Jane Austen. Later he wrote to James Edward Austen, the nephew of Jane, "My late venerable uncle…said in so many words that he was in love with her, although he qualified his confession by saying it was a boyish love. As this occurred in a friendly and private conversation, I feel some doubt whether I ought to make it public". It was written of Jane and Tom by a contemporary family member that, "The one thing certain is that to the last year of his life she was remembered as the object of his youthful admiration".

Yet, what if Tom had a little more courage in 1796? What if Jane Austen had married Tom Lefroy, the mind is flooded with possibilities. It is difficult to imagine what Tom felt parting from Jane in January 1796. It was said that Madame Lefroy cut short his holiday because of his conduct towards Jane and it was also said that she intervened to end their romance for financial reasons. Although Tom was shocked, duty to his family had to take precedence over his love for Jane. He was young, perhaps lacking in courage, and weighed down with family expectations. He was not free now but there would come a time when Tom Lefroy, the eldest son would be rich and powerful and eminent enough to make his own choices. The question is would Tom Lefroy have been able to cope with a genius like Jane Austen? As he got older his nature seemed more austere and his character seemed strict and unyielding.

After their marriage in 1799 Tom and Mary made their home in Leeson Street, Dublin, and their nine children were born there. His work as Barrister and later as Judge often took him away from home and it is said that the more he achieved in his work, the more pious he became. Apparently, he wrote to Mary every day and included a sermon to be read for each day of his absence. How would Jane react to this? How did she react when she heard that he had his first daughter born in June 1802, baptised 'Jane Christmas' Lefroy? Most likely he had Jane and the Christmas season of 1795 in mind.

Tom Lefroy attained excellence in his career, and became a bencher of the King's Inns in 1819. He entered Parliament in 1830 as one of the members for the University of Dublin. In 1852 he reached the zenith of his career becoming Lord Chief Justice of Ireland at the age of seventy-six. In 1837 he built a beautiful mansion in Carrigglas Co. Longford. He was opposed to Catholic Emancipation which became law in 1829, and founded a society to send missionaries into traditional Catholic areas. During the great famine in Ireland between 1845-1847, which reduced the Irish population from eight million to 4 million, Tom witnessed their starvation and suffering. One hopes he was a man of compassion and helped them.

The following lines are from a song by Thomas Moore who was a contemporary of Tom at Trinity College in 1795. The song may have been known to Tom and reminded him of that Christmas season in Hampshire all those years ago, when with careless abandon he had courted Jane Austen;

'Oh' The days are gone when beauty bright
My hearts chain wove
When my dream of life, from morn' till night
Was love, still love
New hope may bloom and days may come,
Of milder calmer beam,
But there's nothing half so sweet in life as
Loves young dream.

CHAPTER 11

SWEET CORK OF THEE

"Partly coloured like the people, red and white is Shandon Steeple" (an old Cork City jingle)

While on holiday in Cork, I visited the town of Cove in Cork Harbour, my sister Theresa came with me. Many of the ships Jane's brother Charles had sailed on spent time here. On to the Maritime museum we went but alas, disappointment, there was no exhibits of their era. Unexpectedly a kind member of staff pointed to a steep hill telling us that the 18th Century Admiralty House was at its top.

With high hopes and a hard climb on a hot summer's day, we arrived at this architectural gem. A nun answered the door but on hearing of our quest she shook her head. Still, she invited us for a cup of tea in the garden. Moments later I was gazing downwards with a magnificent bird's eye view of Cork Harbour. This feast for the eyes surpassed all my expectations for the day. Here for the first time I had seen Cork Harbour in all its beauty.

Many times I travelled home to Cork by ship. On a calm night as it entered the harbour I would go up on deck and stay there until we reached the river Lee. There was a kind of reverence in the air. It would be around five in the morning. The lights from the harbour villages would still be lit. It was a wondrous sight and a wonderful moment to be alive. The Admiralty had great vision to build this house on the best vantage point for the view of Cork harbour.

'Moored in the Cove of Cork'
I have slumbered in Palm Groves by clear running streams,

And the Wild Groves of Blarney came haunting my dreams.
I have listened to bells on the soft summer wind,
But the sweet bells of Shandon were dear to my mind
There is nought in the land of the slave or the free,
Like the green hills of Cork, and my home by the Lee.

"What a fine fellow Charles is, to deceive us into writing two letters to him at Cork!" Jane wrote to her sister Cassandra on the 1st Sept 1796. "I admire his ingenuity extremely, especially as he is so great a gainer by it" (Lt 4)." From this it is clear that Jane wrote to her brother, Charles, sending the letters to Cork. She wrote again to Cassandra on the 15th Sept. 1796, "So - his royal Highness Sir Thomas Williams has at length sailed - ; the Papers say 'on a cruise'. But I hope they are gone to Cork, or I shall have written in vain" (Lt 6). Britain and France were at war during this time and if a ship was 'on a cruise' it was a term for a secret mission.

Fast forward to the year 1816 when, in her last novel *Persuasion*, Jane mentions 'Cork'. "What a great traveller you must have been, ma'am!" said Mrs. Musgrove to Mrs. Croft. Mrs. Croft replies with "Pretty well, ma'am, in the fifteen years of my marriage...I have crossed the Atlantic four times, and have been once to the East Indies...besides being in different places about home - Cork, and Lisbon, and Gibraltar. But I never...was in the West Indies. We do not call Bermuda or Bahama, you know, the West Indies" (PER p 70).

In *Persuasion*, Mrs. Croft, Admiral Croft's wife, describes fifteen years of happy married life living at sea or on 'stations' abroad most of the time, stating that "nothing can exceed the accommodations of a man-of-war" (PER p 70) She was referring to the main battle ships of the navy which had mostly three decks and carried between 32 and 144 guns. The places she visits and the routes she travels were once visited by Jane Austen's 'sailor' brothers, Frank and Charles, who would have visited Cork countless times. In *Persuasion*, Jane is showing her feeling for the navy and Cork, evocative of her youth when she was intensely absorbed in her brothers' maritime adventures.

In Jane's earlier novel, *Mansfield Park*, Fanny Price has a visit from her brother William, a young midshipman. 'Young as he was, William had already seen a great deal. He had been in the Mediterranean - in the West Indies - had been often taken on shore by the favour of his Captain, and in the course of seven years had known every variety of danger, which sea and war together could offer' (*MP* p 236). In these lines Jane is almost certainly writing about her younger brother Charles and the 'seven years' are from 1794 to 1801 when he was, for some of this time, under the patronage of a Captain Williams.

Captain Williams had become part of the Austen family through his marriage to the beautiful Jane Cooper, a niece of Mrs Austen. Cassandra and Jane Austen shared school days with Jane Cooper at Reading and later at Southampton. Here, they all became very ill with an infection and their mothers came to bring them home. Sadly, Mrs Cooper caught the infection and died. Consequently, eleven-year-old Jane Cooper spent much time with her cousins at Steventon and the three young girls became great friends. During this time, Jane Austen began writing and dedicated her short comical novel, *Henry and Eliza*, to her young cousin (*MW* pp 33/39). In July 1792, on the Isle of Wight, Jane Cooper met Captain Williams. After a brief engagement, they were married at Steventon Church with Jane and Cassandra as bridesmaids. Captain Williams then took Jane's younger brother Charles under his wing and became his patron. (Tucker p 181). In 1791, at the age of twelve, Charles Austen followed in the footsteps of his brother Frank and enrolled as a pupil at the Naval Academy, Portsmouth. (*Jane Austen* D. Nokes p 122). At fifteen he left to become midshipman aboard HMS *Daedalus*, under the command of Captain Williams.

In June 1796, while serving under Captain Williams on the *Unicorn* and patrolling Irish waters Charles 'was involved in an exciting sea chase and captured 'a prize', the French frigate *La Tribune* (*Jane Austen's Sailor Brothers*). These were 'exciting times', as such enemy action and the capture of 'prizes' were obliquely referred to in his correspondence. A 'prize' was the enemy ship and its cargo, a sort of legalised piracy, which meant good profits for the victors. Captain Williams was knighted for this exploit but records of the incident are vague because of the security risk and fear of espionage. In March 1797 Charles faced conflict with the Dutch battleship *Brutus* and was made a lieutenant in December at the age of 18.

Jane writes passionately about the Navy in *Mansfield Park* and

Persuasion and she brings in many incidents of Charles' young days when he became a midshipman and began his naval career. In *Mansfield Park*, William Price, about to become midshipman on the Thrush, conveys his thoughts on 'schemes for...action...speculations upon prize money' (*MP* p 375). In *Persuasion*, Captain Wentworth describes the 'pleasant days' when he 'made money' while on the Laconia: "A friend of mine, and I, had such a lovely cruise together off the Western Islands" (*PER* p 67) and "had not made less than twenty thousand pounds" (*PER* p 75). In *Persuasion* Sir Walter is in debt. Mr Shepherd suggests that he let Kellynch Hall "The war is over and rich naval officers will be coming ashore wanting a home." and a rich admiral might "come in our way". Sir Walter replies that Kellynch Hall would be "the greatest prize of all" (*PER* p 17).

In 1801 Charles was stationed in the Mediterranean and had sent home gold chains and topaz crosses for his sisters from prize money earned during his stay. In *Mansfield Park* William Price brought back from Sicily a gold and amber cross for his sister Fanny (*MP* p 254). What happened out in the Atlantic to the French and Spanish crews, before the prizes were brought to Portsmouth, Gibraltar or Cork, was unclear. They were either taken prisoners; or jumped from their ships. 'The tragic nature of the coast was reinforced by the terrible pontoons on which, a stone's throw from the finest bathing resorts, the bodies of prisoners rotted slowly' (*Lure of the Sea* p 241). Jane worshipped her brave and fearless Charles, but her novels do not touch on the cruel side of his life at sea. Just a sentence that he 'had known every variety of danger which sea and war together could offer' (*MP* p 236)

Cork, the primary base

In the years between 1795 and 1797 Charles accompanied Captain Williams on trips ashore while serving on the *Unicorn*. Most of this time was spent in the coastal waters close to Ireland with protracted stays in and around Cork, the primary base. The Captain's Logs tell of frequent revictualling from Cork, plus a lengthy refitting of sails and masts and various troop movements there. Jane's letters to Cassandra reveal that security matters appeared to mask much of the ship's activities, but below are details of the log of the *Unicorn*.

The Unicorn - Captain Thomas Williams - ref. ADM 51/1183
July 1795 to March 1797

Spithead..Lizard..Cornwall
19th July 1795 Cork
29th July 1795 to Ballycotton Island off entrance to Cork Harbour to Cape Clear...

The Unicorn spends the next whole month of August patrolling the Irish coast...then to

Barra Island...St Kilda...N. Ronaldsay
24th September.Inishon Head
26th September...Moored in Cove of Cork until 5th October 1795...then to North Isles and Scotland

End of 1795 beginning of 1796 based at Spithead

25th February 1796 ...single anchor in Cork Harbour... 26th February 1796...Cork Head...to Cape Clear...Finisterre

4th April Cove Cork Tuesday 5th April 1796...Moored in Cork Harbour until Thursday 12th April...Cape Clear...Ushant Thursday 21st April 1796...Cork Head Friday 22nd April 1796 Ballycotton...

13th May through to the 19th May 1796...Moored in the Cove of Cork at single anchor

13th June 1796 Ballycotton 14th June Moored in Cove of Cork.

After leaving Cork in June 1796 details of the sailings of the *Unicorn* are obscure. On Thursday 23rd June until Monday 27th June its whereabouts are unclear. Captain Williams reports firing several shots at a strange sail on shore. Where is the *Unicorn* in July? The next mention is the 26th July at the Bill of Portland. We know from the log of the *Unicorn* that it was moored east of Cork Harbour, in Ballycotton, where men were skilled in boat building and its offshoot mending industries. The famous town of Kinsale, south west of Cork Harbour, was also in the log of Captain Williams ship when Charles was midshipman, and delighted him with its historic loyalty to the Stuarts, something to relate to Jane who had a fondness for them. Its strategic site was highly suitable for the building of several forts for troops supporting the Stuart Kings James I and Charles I. The splendid Charles Fort played its part in a great event in Kinsale's history, the arrival of another Stuart King, the deposed James II in 1689. The nearby Desmond Castle was important for centuries as a storage depot for the wine and spirit imports from the continent, but in the 1790s French prisoners from the naval wars were detained there. As the *Unicorn* sailed west towards Cape Clear it passed

Courtmacsherry with its flourishing boat trade, and the historic Castlefreke with its panoramic view of the coast which enabled the spotting of enemy ships.

The Cove of Cork - "That other great seaport"

When the *Unicorn* 'moored' in the Cove of Cork on the 14th June it had entered to what Prime Minister Pitt referred to as 'that other great seaport' Cork Harbour. Natural and extensive it was and is one of the most aesthetically beautiful and safest harbours in the world. Its coat of arms 'Statio Bene Fida Carinis' translates as 'safe haven for ships'. It surely presented a dramatically attractive panorama in this golden age of sailing, similar to that which Jane herself described in *Mansfield Park*, inspired by her visits to Portsmouth and her sharing her brothers' enthusiasm for the sea. 'The day was uncommonly lovely. It was really March; but it was April in its mild air, brisk soft wind, and bright sun, occasionally clouded for a minute; and everything looked so beautiful under the influence of such a sky, the effects of the shadows pursuing each other, on the ships at Spithead and the island beyond, with the ever-varying hues of the sea now at high water, dancing in its glee and dashing against the ramparts with so fine a sound' (*MP* p 409).

Cork was the gateway to the south of Ireland with a narrow entrance to its Harbour. On its west was Crosshaven Hill and the adjoining headland where from the sentinel Rams Head (Camden Fort later) a view of all of Cork Harbour could be seen. One of its Islands was called Spike Island where convicts were imprisoned while awaiting transportation to Botany Bay. In 1791 the *Queen* was the first ship to take Irish prisoners, mostly political, from Spike Island to Sydney Harbour, Australia. Later, mass exportation of Irish prisoners to the penal colonies took place. The largest island in Cork Harbour was the Great Island with the town of Cobh (Cove) nestled on it southern shores. High up on a hill above it, was Admiralty House, first built in 1765 from where the Admiral could co-ordinate the vast naval operations, signalling to the hundreds of ships anchored in the harbour. Also, balls and gatherings would be hosted here and the young Charles Austen noted for his looks and style, very likely accompanied Captain Williams to such social events, when the *Unicorn* was moored in the 'Cove of Cork' for short spells in 1795 and 1796.

The Cove of Cork provided amazing sights in the 18th Century. In the peacetime of 1790 the French consul wrote 'In the port are seven or eight warships, their flags deployed'. John Carr wrote in 1806 'as the ships lie safe from every storm, and the houses about it in the form of a crescent are not inelegant, the Cove of Cork suggests pleasant ideas. The harbour being crowded with vessels, and not a few of them men-of-war when I was there. I felt a kind of self-importance arising from the thought that the tonnage and number of ships belonging to Britain…is four times greater than those of all the nations in the world put together. In times of peace the flags of every nation may be seen waving in her harbour…which is perfectly safe, and capable of affording complete protection to the whole navy of England from every wind that blows. Ships from England, bound to all parts of the West Indies, put in here, and in one year, no less than two thousand vessels have floated upon its bosom' (*The Stranger in Ireland* p 257 J. Carr).

From 1788 onwards Cork was significant as a key base for the cross-Atlantic trade with the Northern American territories and the recently independent American states. It was also vulnerable to French interference of the discontented and disenfranchised Irish population. England went to war with Revolutionary France in 1793 and Ireland was in danger. Cork, with its huge accumulation of navy stores had to be defended as it was a nucleus for the maintenance of the British naval network. Naval documents from this turbulent age of sea warfare underline how crucially important Cork was. The possibility of France invading Ireland meant lengthy periods of 'cruising' by the Navy.

Cork and the Battle of Trafalgar

On July 19th 1805 Admiral Collingwood sent a letter from the Dreadnought to Nelson that he considered Ireland as the "real meek and butt of all their operations" - the invasion of Ireland as the aim of Villeneuve tactics. On the 26th July 1805 Admiral Marsden sent a letter from the Admiralty office, to Nelson telling him that he would receive 'intelligence…by a fast sailing vessel' from Rear Admiral Drury 'commanding His majesty's ships and vessels at Cork' if any part of the Enemy's squadron was sighted. These two letters were sent just three months before the Battle of Trafalgar, focusing attention on the possibility that Villeneuve and the French Fleet could invade Cork. Alas, Villeneuve raced out into the Atlantic and Cork was spared. Three months later the Battle of Trafalgar was fought.

The Croppy Boy.

Leading up to the 1798 rebellion young Irishmen willing to fight for their country's independence distinguished themselves by having their hair cropped in the new French style. They were called "Croppies". Songs like *The Croppy Boy* were written and sung, and are still sung today. Many of these young men were imprisoned at Geneva Barracks near Passage not far from the coast of Cork. Around this time, Charles had his hair cropped. He was dissatisfied in serving on the *Scorpion,* a small vessel, and there may have been a hint of rebellion as much as practicality or fashion in his gesture. Also, it is entirely feasible when Charles became a 'Croppy' he manifested latent radical tendencies. Jane wrote to Cassandra that their brother Edward who was ill at the time, would not approve "of Charles being a crop...conceal it from him...it might fall on his spirits and retard his recovery" (Lt 18, January 1799).

Cork City, I have slumbered

Corkonians were tolerant of intermarriage and flouted the Statute of Kilkenny (1367). The growth of trade and prosperity encouraged peaceable, cultural, religious and national integration in Cork. In 1760 Cork City ranked as one of the most important cities of Europe. It had 60,000 citizens, to compare with Liverpool and Birmingham who had 30,000 each and Glasgow 26,000. Over the centuries it had developed into a great trading centre and was at the height of its commercial success in the 1790's.

What was the pink and pearly city of Cork like around the year 1796? Perhaps Captain Williams and the 17-year-old Charles Austen did visit it. They may have hired horses from one of the various harbour locations, as Charles had done some years later when he surprised Jane by arriving at Steventon in a Gosport Hack to make the ball that night (Lt 27). But if they took the boat from the Harbour and sailed up the river Lee they would have seen the city of Cork at its best.

John Carr drew several illustrations of Cork City around the year 1800 and from them it is clear that Cork was an elegant city. As

William Thackeray wrote of Cork in the 1840s: 'A most opulent and beautiful city. I do not know a town to which is an entrance more beautiful, commodious and stately. Passing by numberless handsome lodges and, nearer the city, many terraces in neat order...In the river...some hundreds of ships were lying'. The handsome lodges were the grand houses high up on the hills on the right bank of the river Lee and could be seen as a ship sailed nearer the city. Several of these houses had the prefix 'Lota' to their name and many were built in the 18th Century reflecting the successful trading life of the City. On the left bank of the river, at the water's edge, was Blackrock Castle, originally built in 1582 to guard Cork's merchant fleet.

As the river Lee nears the city it opens its two arms and spreads them on either side of the land. So there is the South channel and North channel and four river banks. Then the river closes its arms and continues upstream making Cork City an island from its inception. Arriving by ship Charles might have heard the melodious bells of Shandon, and seen its tower visible from all around the city. It has four sides or faces, two of sandstone and two of limestone with four mighty clocks and perched on top is a glorious 'pepper pot' steeple. Shandon is, and was, always loved by the people of Cork who believe the sound of its bells is the music of Cork City. In the 1800s Father Prout who spent his childhood in Cork composed the well-loved song *The Bells of Shandon* immortalising its tower and the sound of its eight bells. He is buried in its church yard.

The bells of Shandon that sound so grand on the pleasant waters of the River Lee. (He wished it sung with the resonance of a dozen pianofortes "to rouse the heart and elevate the souls of the hearers, giving the glorious peelings of the bells altogether" *This City of Cork* Pettit S.F. p 298)

Built on a marsh the beautiful city had its greatest facelift between 1750 and 1800, when impressive building projects were underway, not only the filling in of the waterways to create wide new thoroughfares like Patrick St. and Grand Parade, but also building elegant showpiece housing on the North and South Malls. Many of the deeds of these properties include mooring rights from that time.

The almost vertical Patrick's Hill with its beautiful Mansions meet the newly built Patrick's Bridge which ends with the graceful curve of Patrick St. The river Lee and its waterways gave Cork it's effortless elegance.

The passionate merchants

Cork had always been a merchant city but in the 18th Century its citizens became passionate about trade and Cork blossomed for the following 200 years. The immense volume of trade meant that the streets and waterways were busy and always bustling, with horses and carts taking provisions to the ships at any one of the many quays. The mass marketing of butter was developed and created great wealth. Other industries like brewing (Beamish and Crawford 1792). and meat products with associated industries like soap, glue and tanning flourished. Also, the traders and craftsmen were linked to the maintenance and provision of the ships themselves. This wealth in turn promoted the demand for luxury goods, like fine glass, silverware and wine imports as the local building of grandiose houses on picturesque riverside malls demanded the associated lifestyle.

This privileged lifestyle included attending grand functions at the Mansion House where the Lord Mayor resided. It was here that the 4th Earl Fitzwilliam (Mr Darcy's prototype) received the freedom of the City of Cork in 1795. The rich merchants enjoyed socialising here, and at other such venues as the Exchange in Castle street which had an arcade of shops at ground level where the 'ladies of fashion' could be supplied with all their needs and tastes. The spacious rooms upstairs were used by day for business and by night for glittering grand balls. Cork people were renowned for their love of music and theatre, and had their own Theatre Royal in George Street (GPO stands on its grounds now), where the latest plays and operettas were performed to all classes. Jane Austen would have enjoyed all this.

The architecture of Cork City

Apart from its much loved 'Shandon' and its beautiful domestic architecture displaying various architectural gems Cork city had no great public buildings to boast of, but if Charles Austen, who was a religious man, had the opportunity of visiting the city, he may have seen St. Finbarr's Cathedral (begun 1735) or the nearby Catholic church called the 'South Chapel'. He may have seen the oldest building in Cork City, The Red Abbey Tower built around the year 1490 as part of an Augustinian Priory. In the Northside he might have visited St. Anne's Shandon, or the 'North Chapel' the Catholic church nearby.

Finbarr and Cork City

In the 7th Century, Finbarr (St. Finbarr) a monk came from a place called Gouganbarra, County Cork and built an abbey and school beside the south arm of the river Lee. The Vikings invaded later and physically destroyed most of the 'city' but the traditions of Finbarr's scholarship lived on. The Normans conquered Cork in 1172, and built walls around the city with two small bridges over its two arms, the North Gate and the South Gate bridges. Each bridge was extended to have its own castle and gaol. The Normans gave Cork the lifestyle of a European city.

The brave 'saucy city' and its allegiance to the Stuarts

Cork City was labelled the 'saucy city' by the Stuart king James I (1566-1625) and he sent over his lord deputies to demand its submission. It's citizens rose to the occasion and gave him the nickname Queen Jamie (*His. of Cobh* p 32). Jane Austen's loyalty for the Stuart Cause was perhaps echoed by her brother Charles, and would have delighted in Cork City's allegiance to the Stuarts. But Corkonians paid a terrible price for this allegiance in the 'Siege of Cork' 1690. The armies of the dethroned James II and his replacement William of Orange fought for their kings on Irish soil. William's army under the Duke of Marleborough set out from Portsmouth with a fleet of 82 ships and a thousand men. In Sept. 1689, they occupied the fort at Haulbowline. They were supplemented by 4,000 Dutchmen under the Duke of Wurtemberg. Reaching Cork City and marching down Evergreen Street they conquered Elizabeth Fort and blasted the walled city of Cork. The victims were buried in a mass grave in Christ Church Lane. The following year the Treaty of Limerick saw the exile of those implicated in this rebellion against the conquering British. The Stuart dynasty was no more, and the "Flight of the Wild Geese" from Cork Harbour meant the forced dispersion overseas, often in dangerously overcrowded sailing conditions of those implicated.

The Cork Gaol

In 1789, a Quaker by the name of John Howard visited a Cork gaol to find prisoners dead and others dying either victims of alcohol or violence. In 1807 the Duke of Wellington, visited the city and when shown the site selected for the new gaol which was largely flooded, is reported as having remarked, "I suppose this is been done from motives of economy to save the hangman's fee, for if you do not choose to hang them you may drown them". Afterwards another site was chosen. Gallows Green outside the city was the scene of many public executions, quartering and gibbeting.

Many celebrated and notorious characters came to Cork

Edmund Spenser (1552-1599) lived for a time in North Main Street in the City and wrote some verses of his poem the *Faerie Queene* there.

Sir Francis Drake in 1589, with a small squadron of five ships of war, was chased into Cork harbour by a superior fleet of Spaniards. He ran into Crosshaven and moored his ships behind the shelter of Currabinny Hill in a safe inlet. The Spaniards sailed up the harbour not knowing about Crosshaven and lost sight of Sir Francis and he and his men were unharmed. The inlet became known as Drake's Pool.

Some of the historical characters Jane mentions in her *History of England* had been to Cork.

Sir Walter Raleigh (1552-1618) who Jane wrote that she 'has nothing to say in praise of' (*HOE MW* p 148) lived at Myrtle Grove, Youghal and received 42.000 acres for favours to the British Crown.

Oliver Cromwell (1599-1658) the ferocious puritan, who Jane named as a Villain in her Gang (*HOE MW* p 149) was booed by Cork women as he entered Christ Church in the heart of the city in December 1649.

Nano Nagle, the Lady with the lantern - a worthy native of Cork.

Jane Austen had a love for education. How would she have viewed the inspirational, educational pioneering work of Nano Nagle? Long before Madame de Genlis opened her dwelling in Paris to educate Aristocratic children, and before Maria Edgeworth published *Essays on Practical Education* and her father set up the school in Edgeworthstown, Nano Nagle was opening schools in rooms and attics in Cork City to educate destitute children, especially girls. She was born in County Cork in 1718 to an aristocratic Catholic family of

Norman Descent, but was denied a Catholic education because of the penal laws. At the age of ten she was sent to school in Paris with her sister, and on finishing her education remained there to enjoy the jubilant lifestyle of the city. Yet the image of the poverty in Ireland never left her. She came back to Cork City where using her own wealth, began her life's work. In the 1750s and early 1760s Nano lived dangerously managing to evade the authorities while educating the children of the poor. Harsh penal laws excluded the Catholic population from education and teaching of the Catholic faith meant a large fine plus jail for three months for each offence. Soon Nano's work expanded to providing food and medicine for the sick and needy. She founded an order of nuns and on Christmas Eve in 1775, the year Jane Austen was born, Nano and her companions opened their first Presentation Convent school in the South side of the City. She died at the age of 65 in 1784. I am one of Nano Nagle's successes as I was educated in her second school in the North side of Cork City. It is amazing that both Nano Nagle and Maria Edgeworth had the education of women at heart. (Edmund Burke who was one of the great political philosophers of the 18th Century was a cousin of Nano Nagle. He became a distinguished parliamentarian at Westminster. He spent much of his young days in Ballygriffin House her childhood home).

Cork was very much involved in the abolition of the Slave Trade

Cork was bound to encounter the Slave trade. Literature concerning the plight of the slaves was frequently circulated in Cork. *The Negro's Complaint*, a ballad, was an example. A Cork newspaper had a case investigated by CASS which resulted in freeing slaves from a ship in Cork Harbour. In 1792 a Mr. Edwards of Castle St. issued a pamphlet, An Essay on the Slave Trade, listing its horrors, showing the vice of consuming West Indian products, and also showing the certainty of abolition by the disuse of them. Cork had a confectionery shop that produced sweets not made from West Indian sugar but made from East Indian sugar. Cork was very much involved in the abolition of the Slave Trade. The Cork Quakers abstained from the products of slave labour and continued to work for Negro freedom after the Slave Trade was abolished in 1807.

Jane Austen had an awareness of the slave trade and its horrors, as can be detected in her novels. In *Mansfield Park* Sir Thomas Bertram goes to his estate in Antigua 'for the better arrangement of his affairs' (*MP* p 32) and on his return Fanny loved to hear her "uncle talk of the West Indies" and asked him "about the slave trade" while his own daughters were disinterested in the subject (*MP* pp 197/8). One day in Bristol with my son Paul and his family, having tea in a Methodist hall, I read that the first slave trader hailed from Bristol and his name was Hawkins. In *Emma*, Mr Elton marries Augusta Hawkins from Bristol. A coincidence?

In conclusion

My vision had grown since that day in Cork City all those years ago, when walking along Patrick Street in the rain, I found *Persuasion*, Jane's last novel. She touches on Cork, but as the ample evidence provided by the Captain's Logs shows, Cork and its magnificent, plentiful coastline was the territory of her much-loved brother Charles at a seminal point in his career and was later also well known to Frank. Regrettably little of the correspondence of this time survives, but clearly Cork would have been significant as a safe-haven near home, where the brothers returned to after exciting sea chases out in the vast Atlantic, where letters were sent and received from Jane and other family members reaffirming their all-important close family contact.

Prints, paintings and documents of this time enable us to put together a picture of a thriving city, a centre of commerce and trade and prominent on the social celebrity and arts scene. Its beautiful harbour was paramount as a strategic naval junction of the world. Jane must surely have been interested to hear of such a place which held such relevance in the life of her dear brother Charles, and was of national consequence in contemporary affairs. It would be fascinating to know how much he chose to tell of such things, but we know of Jane's love of authentic detail, and so it is hard not to imagine her eager for a description of his travels. Cork city would have offered a feast of discovery, a polyglot hubbub presenting a spectrum from the glamorous and exotic to the mundane and brutal. There, the stylish excesses of the rich contrasted with the misery of economic exploitation and political repression, the desolation of soon to be exiled prisoners and disgruntled wretches press ganged into a life at sea. How did such extreme inequality fit in with the scholarly decency one imagines would circumscribe the life of a Hampshire country vicar and his daughters at that time?

CHAPTER 12

CONCLUSION

Without my family and friends, this book would never have been written. Even now I have a sense of bewilderment with it all. Shakespeare's quote comes to mind, "There's a divinity that shapes our ends rough hew them as we will" and that is true for me. One thing I can say is that I did not retire from life to write it. In fact, quite the opposite is true. The excursions with friends and family to the places of Jane's life and novels were the fuel that gave me the drive to write. On most occasions, we met many caring and kind people who shared their time to help us. I learned fresh facts which were not found in the history books.

Travelling in Jane's footsteps

The first 8 years of writing this book were as if I had become a time traveller. I went where Jane or the characters of her novels had been. Chawton and the lovely Hampshire countryside beckoned several times. Sitting in its garden I imagined Jane looking out of the window watching the mail coaches on their way to Winchester. My sisters returned to London once more for a short few days. 'What is happening with Jane Austen today?' Margaret would say. She was away from her daily cares of running a shop and her carefree mood would set the tone for our adventures. On our visit to the West End, we walked down Harley St. where Mrs John Dashwood "fell into violent hysterics" on hearing of her brother's engagement to Lucy Steele" (*SS* p 259), and to Pall Mall where in a stationer's shop

Colonel Brandon heard that John Willoughby was soon to marry the heiress, Miss Grey (*SS* 199).

I went with my niece to Weymouth where Frank Churchill and Jane Fairfax became secretly engaged in *Emma* and where so many lovely Georgian houses can still be seen. To Brighton with my son John where Lydia and Wickham eloped from in *Pride and Prejudice*. With my brother to Portsmouth to see the ramparts where Fanny and her family walked along in *Mansfield Park*. It seemed a dreary place to me. On the ferry to the Isle of Wight a member of the ship's crew pointed out to us the area of Spithead which was well known to Jane's brothers. Another excursion with my friend Kathy to the magnificent Cathedral of Winchester where Jane is buried in one of its naves. The words on her grave say it all; 'The benevolence of her heart, the sweetness of her temper, and the extraordinary endowment of her mind obtained the regard of all who knew her, and the warmest love of her intimate connections'.

Ireland and my desire to see where the characters I wrote about had lived

I had been to Dublin numerous times but now I sought out Dorset St. the birthplace of Sheridan and was stunned with the grandeur of Leinster House, once the townhouse of the Fitzgerald family. I visited the village of Blackrock where Lord Edward went to school. I even got a glimpse of Carton, the Fitzgerald home in Co. Kildare before heading for Dun Laoire where I boarded the ferry for Holyhead, North Wales. Millions of passengers have travelled across the Irish sea over the centuries just like Maria Edgeworth did in pursuit of fame. The 4th Earl Fitzwilliam did, humiliated after his 1795 fiasco, and Lord Edward Fitzgerald, perhaps to meet his cousin Charles Fox in London and as Tom Lefroy did to lose his heart to Jane.

Domestic Architecture

I could have written a history of 18th Century Domestic Architecture alongside this book as I visited so many Georgian houses, Irish Houses, English Houses, both city and country houses, houses by the sea and away from the sea. Everywhere I went there were Georgian Houses, lovely surprises but sadness too as sometimes these beautiful works of architecture needed loving attention. In the

City of Cork almost hidden away behind some trees, high up on a hill overlooking the River Lee is the picturesque Fort William House. Bernadette and I asked for permission to visit this beautiful house and I felt very fortunate to be walking through its rooms, seeing its stylish Georgian furniture and beautiful ornaments, perhaps one time used by the 4th Earl himself. Our visit was a happy and enthusiastic rendezvous.

Killarney, our last outing together

One of my precious memories is of Margaret, Bernadette and myself visiting Killarney and while sharing a meal in the garden of a restaurant, surprise surprise, Jane was mentioned. I told them of a book with the title *The Lake of Killarney* which Jane alluded to in one of her letters where "Edward was reading the Lake of Killarney and twisting himself about in one of our great chairs" (Lt 59). We agreed to search for a copy of the book and went to a second-hand book shop nearby. The hilarity began and, though we never found the book, we had great fun in that Aladdin's cave leaving with a pair of bookends, postcards and a poetry book. Unbelievably, we were three cancer patients at the time, each of us receiving treatment. I felt unbearably happy that day in 1999 and little did I know it would be our last outing together. They were with me since the start of my exciting journey and had so lovingly accompanied me on my excursions, 'happy days'. Margaret saw the Millennium in before she passed away and Bernadette followed in 2003. The lines between Cork and London were no longer buzzing with laughter.

So, in 2004, life had changed and I struggled with the book. My brother who was himself grieving for our sisters was a great help and became my critic. But the excitement and delight had gone. Going from reading the novels of Jane Austen and documenting a handful of citations of Ireland in them to research of her life and family plus the tragic history of Ireland during her lifetime was an extreme challenge. I could not stop reading, I can only imagine I had become obsessive. I looked back and asked myself why was I writing 'the book'. I was digging deep for links and some of those links seemed obscure but because of my incessant reading on everything to do with Jane Austen I saw them clearly even if I could not transmit them clearly to the page.

Kentish Town discovery by Noreen

A friend, Noreen, found an article in a magazine which lead me to a chapel down the road from where I live. On one of its walls there is a plaque dedicated to Charles wife, Frances. Frances came from a prosperous Kentish Town family with the name of Palmer. She was 24 when, in September 1814, she died during childbirth on board Charles's ship the *Namur* at the Nore anchorage at the mouth of the Thames. The baby girl survived for 21 days. Below is the inscription on the plaque:

Stop Passenger and Contemplate,
A Child whom Nature's God had taught the Way,
Her Parents dictates ne'er to disobey
A sister in whom Centered every love
to Charm the Angels in the Realms above,
A Loving Wife, a Parent truly dear,
A Pious Christian and a Friend sincere, …
Sleep on dear fair One, wait the Almighty's will
Then rise unchanged, and be an Angel Still.

Holloway College

I thought about doing a master's degree with the material I had gathered and one day, as I was passing North London College in Holloway, I had an idea. I walked in and asked the receptionist if I could make an appointment to see someone from the Literature Department. "There he is" she said pointing to a man nearby. Luck was with me as I quickly told him of *Jane Austen and the Irish Connection* and instantly he agreed to have me as a student. I asked him how long it would take, "five years" he said. I thought it would be three years but he assured me that I would need five. On the way home it occurred to me that I might not be alive in five years' time, yet here I am, over a decade later, 'hopefully' bringing to a close, 'The Book'.

Canada calling

In January of 2009 I had a call from Deirdre a friend living in Canada, to tell me of her husband's comment to "get on the phone as quickly as possible and tell Julia to write the book about herself and how she discovered things" and this idea appealed to me. For the umpteenth time, I took up my 'pen' again.

Back and forward between Jane and Ireland over the years

Reading Irish History of Jane's time, the 18th Century, I learnt of the Ascendancy and its corruption. It was a sort of enlightenment for me reading the history of Ireland and England in relation to each other. The Irish were the forced victims of English domination who in 1775 held less than 5% of their native land. David Hume (1711-1776) in his *History of England* wrote of the Irish as 'barbaric' and Jane read his book. Yet I could not help returning to the ancient past when before the Norman invasion Ireland had been known as The School of the West and the Island of Saints and Scholars, with women of the calibre of St Brigid of Kildare and St Ita of Limerick, who were renowned for their teaching and integrity.

I could not extol the lyrical prose of Jane Austen's novels enough. They have traditional values at their core. Her plots are realistic and universal with love at their centre. Most of her characters have names associated with her ancestors. They are authentic, set in the family and community and she cares about them as if they were members of her own family. Then, perhaps that gives the reader a feeling of warmth for their own family. Jane's novels will always be cherished because they are about the bedrock of civilization, the family unit. Technology may advance, fashions, food and living conditions may change but what Jane wrote about is timeless.

Although Jane had her family, her friends and her culture, these were not enough for her. I believe it was her faith that completed her life and was a guiding strength in her writing. The Jane Austen I came to know through her literature and the volumes of reading material on her life was a witty individualistic happy light hearted woman. She obviously had compassion for the poor as she reveals on a page of her copy of Goldsmith's *History of England*. She wrote 'Pity the poor who are destitute and the rich that make them so'. Her comment on history in *Northanger Abbey* may echo her slightly cynical outlook on the world and its emphasis on power, "it tells me nothing that does not either vex or weary me. The quarrels of popes and kings with wars or pestilences...the men so good for nothing, and hardly any women at all" (*NA* p 108).

Pivotal times in my discoveries

I was curious to read that Sheridan's play, *The Rivals*, been performed at The Vine Inn, Hampshire after Jane's death in 1817 until I discovered that it had been the inspiration for her *Pride and Prejudice*. Sheridan's *The School for Scandal* is very witty and so are Jane's novels but her characters do not get off so lightly as his do. The fate of the Dashwoods in *Sense and Sensibility* and that of Maria Bertram in *Mansfield Park* are the consequences of greed.

Another amazing fact for me was that Jane had read of the great Irish harper Dennis Hempson (*TWIG* notes p 200) and ingeniously worked facets of his story into her novel, *Emma*.

Then the wonderful surprise of seeing Cork's magnificent harbour from the hill above Cobh, made possible by the kindness of the nun who invited Teresa and myself in to have a cup of tea in the Convent Garden.

Out of the blue I heard of the 'O'Rourkes of Breifne' flagstone. It came about because I went to see Maria Edgeworth's House in county Longford and in the afternoon met my friend Mena and her husband Vincent who drove me to Ballinamuck, the battlefield of the 1798 Rebellion. Later as I shared a meal with them, Mena, whose maiden name was O'Rourke, told me of her home in Leitrim where there was a very ancient flagstone marking the origins of the O'Rourkes of Breifne. As I listened, entranced, she stopped and almost apologetically said to me "you wouldn't know about that" but I did know something and told her that the last High King (Ard Rhi) of Breifne was my favourite hero in Irish history. I was astonished and thrilled at what Mena had revealed and in a roundabout way I attributed this delight to Jane Austen.

The connections with Ireland and Jane Austen in my book have been drawn from evidence in her earliest writing, her six novels, her letters and through her family and I am happy to have discovered such a rich vein of influence that the Irish and Ireland have had on her. Her romance with Tom Lefroy saddened me, but Jane reveals her abiding interest in his actions and accomplishments long after their association ended and Lefroy, when an old man, admitted his youthful love for her. Politics were of immense significance to Jane, and Ireland dominated much of the political scene; the coincidence of names like Fitzgerald in her *Juvenilia* and Fitzwilliam in *Pride and Prejudice* are closely attuned to the contemporary Irish political scene of those years.

The majority of the Irish were experiencing political and religious alienation at this time yet for Jane an Irish cultural presence of music and literature was forged and became permanent in her life. The quality of Irish music in her collection, in manuscript form written out by Jane herself surprised and delighted me. Her idol Richard Brinsley Sheridan was her greatest influence. Maria Edgeworth inspired her and Sidney Owenson's (Lady Morgan) novel *The Wild Irish Girl* perhaps changed her perception of Ireland. I had not heard of any of the above before I had begun my research but they enlarged my world of Irish writers and the theatre, becoming important links in the 'Irish Connection' as did the 4th Earl Fitzwilliam and Tom Lefroy. Jane's knowledge of history inspired me to embrace the histories of Ireland, England, France, and the Americas. The world of the high seas of which her brothers and Ireland were such a part of, made thrilling reading and was intrinsic to my book.

The past seventeen years was a fantastic personal voyage of discovery, this book becoming a kind of romance in my life. It was my renaissance. With a sense of expectation and adventure I set out on a quest to find links between Jane Austen and my native land. Now the quest is over. All those years ago, on a rainy day in Cork I found that book in the bag. I forgot its contents until fate intervened and it re-emerged as *Persuasion*. Out stepped the lady of the book and led me on a voyage of a lifetime.

The end

BIBLIOGRAPHY

18th century Plays, Selected Introduction by John Hampden, Aldine Press, Herts 1964.
A History of Jane Austen's Family, Tucker, George H Sutton Publishing 1998.
A Memoir of Jane Austen, Austen-Leigh, J.E. Oxford University Press 2002.
A Traitor's Kiss, O'Toole, Fintan Granta Books London 1998.
Aristocrats, Tillyard, Stella Vintage 1994.
Belinda, Edgeworth Maria Oxford University Press 1994.
Black Cat in the Window, O Murchu, Liam The Collins Press 1999.
CASS - The Cork Anti-slavery Society, its Antecedents and Quaker Background 1755/1859. Harrison, Richard S. (Cork Historical and Archaeological Society).
Chosen letters of Maria Edgeworth, Barry, F.B. Houghton Mifflin Boston 1931.
Citizen Lord, Tillyard, Stella Chatto & Windus London 1997.
Cork - Historical Perspectives, Jefferies, Henry Alan Four Courts Press 2004.
D McAleer, Jane Austen Society of North America
Essays on Practical Education Printed for R. Hunter 1798
English Stage Comedy 1490-1990, Routledge, Alexander Leggatt London and NY.
General Collection of the Ancient Music of Ireland, W. Power & Co, 1796
In the Shadows, Life in Cork 1750-1930, Mahony, C.O. 1997.
Ireland and the Age of Revolution and Imperialism, (1750-1801).
Irish Melodies, Thomas Moore
Irish Traditional Music, Carson Ciaran The Appletree Press Ltd. 1986.
Jane Austen A Life, Tomalin Claire Penguin Books 1998.
Jane Austen and Maria Edgeworth War of Ideas, (CF. RF. Butler) 1975.
Jane Austen and the Navy, Southam, Brian Hambledon and London, 2000.
Jane Austen and the Peerage, Greene D.
Jane Austen and the Theatre, Byrne, Paula Hambledon and London 2002.
Jane Austen and the Theatre, Gay, Penny Cambridge University Press 2002.
Jane Austen Irony as Defence and Discovery, Mudrick, Marvin 1952.
Jane Austen, Lefroy, Helen Sutton Publishing Ltd. 1997.

Jane Austen's Family, Tucker, George Holbert Sutton Publishing Ltd. 1998.
Jane Austen's Letters, Collected and Edited by R.W. Chapman, Oxford University Press, 1979.
Jane Austen's Literary Manuscripts, Southam, B.C. 1964.
Jane Austen's Music, Gammie & McCulloch, Ian & Derek Corda Music Publications 1996.
Jane Austen's novels A Study in Structure, Wight, Andrew J. Penguin Books Ltd. 1953.
Jane Austen's Sailor Brothers, Hubback, J.H. and Edith C. The Bodley Head 1906.
Lectures on the English Comic Writers 1818, Hazlitt, William Oxford University Press 1907.
Maria Edgeworth and Sir Walter Scott Unpublished letters 1823,' Review of English Studies N.S. ix (1958).
Memoirs of the Life of the Right Honourable Richard Brinsley Sheridan, Moore, Thomas London 1825.
My Aunt Jane Austen Austen, Caroline The Jane Austen Society 1991.
Oliver Goldsmith, Everyman's poetry, Selected and edited by R. L. Mack Orion, London 1997.
Rebels & Informers, Knox, Oliver John Murray 1997.
Romeo and Juliet, Shakespeare, William.
Sheridan's Three Plays, Ratcliff, A.J.J. Thomas Nelson & Sons, Ltd, 1937.
The Age of Improvement, Briggs, Asa Longman Group Ltd 1984.
The American Heritage Book of Indians, American Heritage Publishing Co., Inc. 1961.
The British Theatre, Trussler, Simon, Cambridge University Press 2000.
The Capture of the land, Atkinson, Norman The Whig Club (Folens).
The Complete plays of William Congreve, edited by H. Davis University of Chicago Press, 1967.
The French Revolution, Lefebvre, Georges, Volume II Columbia University Press 1964.
The life and letters of Maria Edgeworth, A.J.C. Hare Educational Boston 1895.
The Life And Poems Of Thomas Moore, Clifford, Brendan Athol Books 1993.
The Lure of the Sea, Corbin Alain Penguin Books 1994.
The Novels of Jane Austen Volume II Pride and Prejudice, Edited by R.W.

Chapman Oxford University Press 1949.
The Oxford Dictionary of Plays, Patterson, Michael Oxford University Press 2005.
The Prizes of War, Corbin Richard
The Reminiscences of Michael Kelly of the King's Theatre and Theatre Royal Drury Lane, (H. Colburn,1826) E. Wikipedia.
The Rights of Man, Paine Thomas 1791.
The Rivals, Sheridan R.B. Edited by A.J.J. Ratcliff, M.A.
The Same Old Story, Curtis, Liz Russell Press Ltd 1998
The School for Scandal, Sheridan, Richard Brinsley .Edited by F.W. Bateson, London A & C Black
The social landscape in Cork in 1737, Insights by Alexander, the Coppersmith.
The Stranger in Ireland, Carr, John 1806.
The Vicar of Wakefield, Goldsmith, Oliver (1766) Minster Classics London 1968.
The Wild Irish Girl, Owenson Sydney (1806) Oxford University Press 1999.
The Works of Jane Austen, Minor Works Collected and Edited by R.W. Chapman Oxford University Press 1963.
This City of Cork 1700-1900, Pettit, Dr.S.F. Studio Publications Cork 1977.
Tom Lefroy and Jane Austen, le Faye, Deirdre Jane Austen Society.
Whig Principles and Party Politics, - Earl Fitzwilliam and the Whig Party 1748-1833.

Jane Austen's writings reference
The Novels of Jane Austen. Volumes I - V. Text based on Collation of the early editions.
by R.W. Chapman. Oxford Press.

Title	Written	First Published
Juvenilia	1789-1792	1912 *
Lady Susan	1793-1794	1912 *
Sense and Sensibility	1795-1797	1811
Pride and Prejudice	1796-1797	1813
Northanger Abbey	1798	1818 *

The Watsons	1804	1912 **
Mansfield Park	1813	1814
Emma	1814	1816
Persuasion	1816	1818 *
Sanditon	1817	1912 **

(* Published after her death. **Unfinished, published after her death)

Jane Austen's Letters
Collected and edited by R.W. Chapman
Oxford University Press

ABOUT THE AUTHOR

Julia was born in Cork City, Ireland, in the 1930's. She was the middle child of 4 girls and one boy. Their mother died when they were all still very young but their father kept the family strong. The children's home life was always happy with lots of singing, dancing and drama. Julia attended Cork's Presentation Convent school where they nurtured her great love of history, maths and literature.

After living some years in London, Julia met Joe Forsythe, who was also from Co Cork. They married and made their home in Kentish Town where they had two boys. Once the boys were old enough, Julia returned to education. She completed a teaching degree and went on to be a successful primary school teacher for many years.

Contact: castlefrekemedia@gmail.com

23858114R00103

Printed in Great Britain
by Amazon